Budgeting

Learn Practical and Simple Budgeting Strategies

(The Limitless Wealth Building Power of the Compound Effect)

Tyrone Long

Published By **Jordan Levy**

Tyrone Long

Budgeting: Learn Practical and Simple Budgeting Strategies (The Limitless Wealth Building Power of the Compound Effect)

ISBN 978-1-7752672-6-3

No part of this guidebook shall be reproduced in any form without permission in writing from the publisher except in the case of brief quotations embodied in critical articles or reviews.

Legal & Disclaimer

The information contained in this ebook is not designed to replace or take the place of any form of medicine or professional medical advice. The information in this ebook has been provided for educational & entertainment purposes only.

The information contained in this book has been compiled from sources deemed reliable, and it is accurate to the best of the Author's knowledge; however, the Author cannot guarantee its accuracy and validity and cannot be held liable for any errors or omissions. Changes are periodically made to this book. You must consult your doctor or get professional medical advice before using any of the suggested remedies, techniques, or information in this book.

Upon using the information contained in this book, you agree to hold harmless the Author from and against any damages, costs, and expenses, including any legal fees potentially resulting from the application of any of the information provided by this guide. This disclaimer applies to any damages or injury caused by the use and application, whether directly or indirectly, of any advice or information presented, whether for breach of contract, tort, negligence, personal injury, criminal intent, or under any other cause of action.

You agree to accept all risks of using the information presented inside this book. You need to consult a professional medical practitioner in order to ensure you are both able and healthy enough to participate in this program.

Table Of Contents

Chapter 1: Budgeting Basics

It can be said that the toughest detail about residing on a finances is sticking to it. We constantly have the brilliant of intentions on the equal time as we create a non-public or circle of relatives fee range but is "without a doubt following the rate range" that is the most hard part of the whole state of affairs. However, I would argue that forming the dependancy is the difficult detail. After that addiction is fashioned, it could be quite clean to stick to it.

We don't all understand what "living on a rate range" includes. When you pay attention that word, what do you right away recollect?

"Having no a laugh."

"Saving all of your coins."

Is that about proper?

Create Some Goals

We are all in particular factors of our lives. Because of this, all of us have tremendous financial duties. Not best that, however we additionally need different things out of our futures.

Some of us want at the way to retire and journey. Some simply want as a manner to live in a tiny house. Other human beings want so that you can have vacations houses that they may visit once they experience the urge to transport round. Some human beings need to shop for our households. Others really want some play cash and cash to stay efficiently in the destiny.

Ask yourself what you need from your life. What varieties of quick term and long term goals do you have got and the manner do you need to financially prepared yourself for the ones desires? Keep in mind that short terms desires should take now not than a 365 days to complete at the same time as an example of an extended-time period purpose might be, "Save for retirement" or "Put away coins for my little one's education."

Do you want to maintain pretty some cash for a new residence? To be organized for kids? Or possibly so you can start your very own commercial business enterprise. How lengthy will it take as a manner to store up the vital price range to make those goals conceivable?

Remember that those dreams aren't set in stone. Things appear in our lives that make us reconsider what we want out of our destiny. You can change the gadgets in this listing as you grow to be older and experience extra subjects.

Pay Close Attention To Your Net Income

One of the maximum crucial pitfalls close to planning out and living on a price variety is growing and following a plan this is inside your income. In a time wherein cloth possessions have grow to be some factor of a status image, we've determined to live out of doors our way. This is one of the important reasons why numerous people are in credit score card debt and might't keep on with a finances or preserve cash.

The first step that you pick out out how a bargain coins you have got were given coming in. Knowing your profits is critical. Some of you could ought to estimate how a exquisite deal you have got got coming in every month due to the fact you very very own your very own organisation, run a settlement or by using using-settlement organization, or due to the reality your earnings fluctuates.

If that is you, make sure which you underestimate how lots profits you convey in each month. I satisfactory propose this as it is easy to overestimate and as a way to purpose your rate variety to be unreasonable and now not viable.

Also don't forget to keep in thoughts your enterprise deductions for taxes, retirement plan, insurance, Social Security, and perhaps spending account allocations.

When You Create Your Plan

When you create your finances plan - and you've placed your commonplace monthly earnings – divide your earnings into large training: consistent spending and variable expenses.

The prices that might fit underneath constant spending should encompass your utilities and bills that don't alternate a whole lot every month. This could encompass your loan, vehicle bills, credit score card bills, ordinary utilities, etc.

The gadgets that could in form below variable costs consist of expenses that alternate every month: entertainment, food (even though this may in shape in each counting on your behavior), gasoline and journey fees, and so on.

I advise that you record those costs for a couple months to look what your tendencies and conduct fall. If you are demanding to get a finances plan organized, I propose which you investigate your financial organisation information. Online banking has made matters particularly smooth nowadays. Some on-line banking money owed even break down your spending for you counting on in that you save.

My online economic employer account does that precise detail; they set up my spending behavior through training. This makes it an awful lot much less complicated to keep tune of wherein my cash goes.

At the minimal, I may manually cut up your spending into 3 one-of-a-kind lessons:

• Needs and requirements

• Savings

• Desires

Needs encompass the fixed and variable expenses which is probably crucial to dwelling a wholesome life. The economic economic savings phase would consist of every emergency price range and retirement. The goals segment ought to cover the entirety else.

Now it's time to customise your budget.

Okay, so you've analyzed your spending conduct. Now it's time to customise a price range. A wonderful trouble that is concurrently obnoxious is the truth that each charge variety want to be personalised. This way which you don't need to be pigeonholed into preserving a price range that doesn't fit your needs (Yay!). However, this additionally technique which you want to art work more difficult to give you the incredible price variety that does (Ooh...).

Okay, now that you've placed out what your consistent spending huge range is, set that aside every month so you will constantly have that cash available for vital charges. What you've got left should be divided up into variable gadgets. This quantity is also a variable in and of itself. If you permit a excessive high-quality amount of factors like clothes, but you comprehend that you want to buy a TV, you could skim a piece from your garments fund and add that in your TV fund.

Making Your Budget.

Creating your actual budget may be done in as little as 4 steps while you've achieved all of that prep art work.

1. Keep a report of your spending and study your effects. Record your spending and function your massive a few specific file theirs as well. I advocate retaining a small pocket e-book and pen with you constantly for one month. In addition to that, maintain a spreadsheet in your computer. Transcribe your.

2. Plan for your subsequent month's spending. If you live with a large distinct, make sure which you plan collectively and that you take all your charges into interest, even if you each have separate bank bills. You don't should keep track of each unique's "preferred" sections. However, it is important to give you a spending cap. When you want to buy some aspect of a certain amount – that allows you to vary with every couple – you could want to defer with each exceptional. Some of you may no longer want to try this. Others sense that it's miles a courtesy to each different. While others but experience that it is critical because of

8

the truth you've got were given got joint debts. My husband and I keep our own information for little spending. However, if some thing charges $a hundred or more, we factor out it to each incredible. If something charges $500 or extra, we communicate it as a set truely so we can offer you with rational and clever alternatives.

3. Look for strategies that you can spend a notable deal a whole lot less. While spending a chunk bit for a long term can upload up, so can saving quite a few cash. Saving simplest a little bit over an extended duration can upload as a high-quality deal as a few high-quality financial financial savings. To do that, do not forget some of the ones alternatives:

1) Shop at a inexpensive grocery hold

2) Buy popular producers

3) Cook at home in region of eating out

4) Entertain at your house instead of going out to a membership or movie

5) Utilize coupons all through earnings

four. You can also find techniques to decorate your earnings. If you've got were given a hobby or talents, you'll be capable of use it to earn some extra cash. Teaching your hobby to others can show to be profitable. You also can promote your wares on an internet shop, or at nearby markets. One wonderful bonus is that you may be in a position to reveal this side pastime proper into a complete-time undertaking if you ever lose your fundamental supply of profits. Handy, huh?

Check Your Spending Habits On A Monthly Basis

Are you sticking on your rate variety? If no longer, in which can be you going off beam and how are you going to restoration that? Take a look at your spending every month and examine it on your fee variety worksheet to peer how topics are going. If you discover which you're regularly going over-finances in some regions out of necessity, you have to recall reducing a few area else to hold matters below manipulate.

Chapter 2: Living Paycheck To Paycheck

Are you bored to death in the constant feeling which you don't have any cash? Living paycheck to paycheck is a actual problem for plenty humans. While a number of the human beings on this rut are low earning households, many are not. Those inside the middle class also can end up entrenched in this cycle.

There is an old saying that you could spend what you earn. Generally, it's far anticipated that you are dwelling indoors your way and assembly all of your monetary responsibilities. At the equal time, you don't have any money left over. As you earn extra cash, you're taking on more prices or luxuries that eat up the greater income. This is how many households fall into the paycheck to paycheck cycle.

Breaking this cycle is viable. You want to have some power of thoughts. You should force your self to deal with not on time gratification. Here are a few recommendations for breaking the cycle.

The Importance of Curbing Spending

Most humans who have hassle making ends meet or running out of coins earlier than the subsequent paycheck hits spend quite a chunk on unnecessary charges. When you cut yet again on a number of the luxuries of life, you could locate that you may shop big quantities of cash. Even if it's far a few factor as simple as deciding on an off logo at the grocery shop, all of these pennies and bucks upload up quickly. Here are a few approaches you may reduce your spending.

1. Limit fast food journeys to 2 consistent with month

2. Buy off manufacturers at the grocery hold

3. Shop thrift shops for clothing in advance than going to department shops

4. Limit enjoyment along with movies and live performance activities to as a minimum one regular with month

5. Cut out or lessen down your cable or satellite tv for pc tv for pc bill

6. Cut lower back on mobile phone utilization and payments

7. Never use payday loans—they charge more than they're well worth

eight. Cut again on riding to the naked minimal to keep on gas

9. Turn up the thermostat in the summer time and down inside the winter—get dressed for the weather in preference to compensating with excessive strength payments

10.   Cut out or lessen back on vices together with soda and cigarettes

11.   Make your desserts as a substitute of purchasing prepackaged cookies and cakes

These are in reality some of the methods you could trim the fats from your spending. Carefully undergo in thoughts in which you spend money which you don't need to spend. Anything you may lessen again is probably beneficial. At the same time, don't deny yourself every pride. You should enjoy like you are making the most of your frugal lifestyle and all of your hard paintings. Denying your self every luxurious all of the time will purpose you to surrender on budgeting.

The Importance of Saving for the Future

One of the maximum crucial issues with residing paycheck to paycheck is which you don't store once more any coins for the destiny. Whether you are looking 5 years in advance or thirty, it's miles essential to maintain at the least a small quantity from every paycheck toward your prolonged-time period desires.

Of route, the massive monetary monetary financial savings aim many humans don't forget is their retirement. If you're greater younger than 40, this event can also seem up to now in the future that it's miles on occasion truely virtually worth disturbing about. However, that is the thoughts-set that is leaving many center-aged adults suffering to figure out what they're going to do once they need to retire. Saving cash on your retirement needs to start at a younger age. If you start early, you can hold a large amount of cash without hurting your common earnings and spending.

Many different topics are towards the prevailing which you could probably need to hold up for. If you're close to any of these activities, otherwise you simply want to be prepared for them inside the destiny, you have to begin saving now. Here are only some.

• A wedding ceremony for yourself or your infant

• Preparing for a child

• College training for a child

• A automobile that you don't have to make payments on

• A down charge on a residence with a purpose to prevent on housing charges

• A nest egg for preservation or alternative of number one domestic system as they age

• A circle of relatives tour that your kids will bear in mind for a whole lifestyles

Saving coins isn't pretty much surviving. It's approximately dwelling. Without saving returned cash for the little things, and the huge matters, that come alongside in existence, you may fail to really revel in them even as they come due to the fact you will be suffering to pay for them. Planning no longer satisfactory continues you prepared for emergencies however additionally decreases strain and increases ordinary happiness.

How Budgeting Helps You Meet Your Goals

Budgeting is an vital step in assisting you meet your goals. Budgeting isn't pretty much being cautious collectively collectively with your cash. You can use budgeting tool to help you plan your profits and spending so that you can deliberately set apart savings. You can use value monitoring to help you trim the fat out of your fee range and note wherein you could make adjustments to decorate your wellknown nice of existence, now and within the destiny. Your long-term monetary desires, further for your quick-term way of existence, can only be determined out via powerful budgeting.

Methods of Budgeting

There are three primary methods to finances. You can budget with the useful resource of every week or pay period, month, or via rate. Budgeting with the beneficial useful resource of charge is the right way to price variety. It is completed by means of way of the usage of the envelope method, so as to be defined quick. Budgeting through consistent with week or pay period will let you forestall the paycheck to paycheck cycle, but works with that mentality on the identical time as you determine to improve your financial behavior. Monthly budgeting is beneficial due to the truth you can see the whole thing you spend monthly at one time. This is vital due to the fact many payments are extremely good paid as quickly as constant with month.

You might also moreover choose out to use a mixture of methods. Sometimes it could be beneficial to have even the maximum easy monthly charge range to apply in aggregate with a weekly price range. It also can help to apply the envelope method, especially if you have trouble putting apart coins for large charges.

Chapter 3: Common Motivation For

Budgeting

Budgeting may be tough when you have no longer superior it proper right right into a addiction. You want to make tough alternatives each day to put into effect your plan well. You may be declining gives from buddies to consume out or to shop for more than one bottle of beer after art work. The hardest challenge of all is to resist vintage conduct that may be inflicting our economic troubles.

In the start, you need to learn how to encourage your self into budgeting. You need to have an excellent motive to hold cash. Most dad and mom art work difficult and sacrifice their instantaneous gratifications for his or her children. Some human beings save up to fund continuing training. You need to don't forget your motive for becoming inexperienced along side your cash.

You want to take a look at your scenario and ask your self why you need to begin budgeting. Here are some reasons that might inspire you to begin this dependancy.

• You might be in a function to buy superb research

By budgeting every day, your family might be capable of shop for things that you generally could possibly not be able to control to pay for. If you recognize the way to test a budget plan, you may be able to maintain coins that you could use for giving awesome opinions for your children.

• You might be organized for all costs, expected or now not

Budgeting permits you to keep a part of your cash for the future. You will be capable of preserve for all your monetary goals given sufficient time. For the unexpected dreams, you have an emergency fund. You can also even avail of offerings as a way to put together you for possible emergencies like accidents and hospitalization.

• You may be capable of save you terrible economic practices that can damage your destiny

One of the vital element requirements of budgeting is consistent consciousness of wherein your cash is going. In the steps to growing your budgeting gadget, you will be instructed to be aware of all your prices. By preserving music of all of your expenses, you may be capable of examine your past prices. You could be capable of discover classes of charges that harm your financial life the maximum. When you have got identified them, you'll be able to prevent the ones terrible spending sports activities from turning into behavior.

• It will hold your circle of relatives happy and contented

A family that budgets is commonly happier and greater contented with life. An effective budgeter is constantly earlier in paying his payments. He does no longer react within the path of fees. He tries to anticipate them and implement strategies to deal with them even supposing the cut-off date remains a ways. If you cope with expenses this way, existence may be masses much less worrying.

• You may be capable of train your youngsters the way to of fee variety, keep and reach their financial goals

If you practice budgeting continuously, you'll be capable of educate your youngsters the monetary thoughts that you comply with via being a high-quality instance to them. You may be succesful to expose them the significance of delayed gratification.

If you want them to learn how to budget properly, you ought to train them the gadget of budgeting. You need to moreover purpose them to privy to the not unusual bad spending practices that might save you them from enforcing their budget plan well.

You must lead them to consciousness on the own family's goals. You ought to moreover display consistency whilst education your budgeting plan, especially at the same time as spending within the front of your kids. If your youngsters see that budgeting may be finished efficiently, they will be more confident with their cash manage capabilities after they grow to be adults.

Discovering Your Motivational Sources

You want to be the simplest to find out what motivates you to finances and keep money. You need to already have a reason for getting this ebook. You need to reawaken that purpose proper now via answering this question:

Why do you need to price variety your coins?

If that doesn't help, you may narrow it down through choosing this form of extra precise questions:

Who motivates you to finances and keep?

What do you want to buy in case you are a achievement in budgeting and saving?

By reflecting on those questions, you will be able to discover your cause for budgeting. You have to write down your motive thru manner of growing a dream announcement. This is a sentence or a paragraph so that you can remind you of your motive for budgeting.

Some people charge variety to buy an pricey buy. Others select to pay large for reviews like journeying to particular places round the area. For some, their supply of motivation is in the direction of domestic. They need to hold to offer their kids with a first rate college training.

When you write your dream u . S ., you want to make it non-public by using the usage of the right phrases. You need to apply unique terms. Instead of announcing:

I want to save for my son's college training.

You need to mention:

I am saving for Michael's college schooling at MIT.

This assertion is a message out of your more youthful self in your older self. By maintaining the kid's name, the message will become extra private whenever you examine it. We moreover modified the annoying used within the announcement. From destiny worrying, we modified it to the prevailing annoying. This signifies which you are already doing the movement. You begin budgeting the instant you make a decision on your intention and write it down. You by no means save you budgeting until your gain your goals.

You want to then write your dream declaration on a couple of portions of paper. You need to tape a assertion to all your credit score score rating playing cards. You have to additionally positioned a replica of this for your pockets. It need to be visible while you open your wallet. This will remind you of what you are saving for, every time you open your pockets. In maximum times, you could make the better economic judgment at the same time as you observe those reminders. This approach will quality fail if you forget about about your dream statements even as you observe them. You want to make it a dependancy to study your assertion out loud while you see it.

Make self-talk a addiction

Most humans buy on impulse. They do now not placed some of idea whilst making purchases. If you typically usually tend to do the equal, you ought to boom a addiction of preventing and thinking in advance than growing a purchase.

You do no longer must make a complex argument out of each purchase. All you want to do is to invite your self this query in advance than every purchase:

Am I creating a financially smart choice?

You want to reply this question by way of of talking to your self out loud. We commonly tend to make wiser alternatives while we pay hobby our reasoning inside the again of our actions. It is also easier to misinform ourselves if we handiest use our mind to justify a buy. We will be inclined to turn out to be ashamed of the lies we inform even as we listen ourselves say it.

Chapter 4: How To Get Over Compulsive

Spending Habits

What is Compulsive Spending?

Have you ever watched the movie Confessions of a Shopaholic? It is a candy, better-than-it-seems rom-com approximately a more younger journalist who is hooked on purchasing. She is trapped within the maze of credit score rating playing playing cards, gathering a debt of extra than $16,000. She lives in a normal terror of debt lenders, she doesn't pay her lease for some months, however she however can't prevent buying.

In the movie, it isn't always noted, but she has a compulsive seeking out sickness (CBD), or oniomania. In workout, due to this someone has obsessive purchasing behavior that deliver negative consequences for them.

Compulsive looking for disease may be brought on via perfectionism, the desire of perceived popularity thru others, the need for manage, or well-known impulsiveness. However, it may moreover be a manifestation of identification looking, social characteristic-gaining hopes, or tension, low self-self perception or melancholy. These reasons do no longer practice to all instances. Not really all and sundry who memories CBD suffers from despair.

For folks which are wealthy, CBD would in all likelihood really seem like an everyday hobby. In many cases it's far. For the ones who've a decent charge variety, this situation can harm their lives. Those who want budgeting the maximum must recall reading more approximately CBD.

The cutting-edge popularity benefit of online shopping for doesn't assist human beings with CBD but alternatively fuels them. They can wander away for hours or days in a web purchasing rabbit hollow, bringing severe consequences to their paintings or private life. Sometimes humans with CBD use online buying as an escape from fact.

The difference among CBD and everyday purchasing is the compulsive, overwhelming desire to shop for and spend towards the better judgment or recognized negative outcomes. Non-addicted customers purchase for the sake of actual need and software program, at the same time as compulsive customers buy for temper-improvement and balancing feelings.

Just like first rate addictions, shopping for disease roots in disappointed emotional desires. Since we realise via now that advertisements usually motive emotions, it's not hard to assume the manner it impacts a person who craves great that need. It looks like capsules – it offers a chunk of remedy when the purchase satisfies the want, however fast the superb outcomes fade. A new, larger dose of satisfaction is probably wanted.

People suffering from CBD anticipate actually as intensely and as often approximately shopping for as an alcoholic approximately the subsequent drink.

Is Compulsive Buying a Mental Health Issue?

We live in a way of life in which cash talks. Better said, gadgets which you buy with cash communicate. Everything encourages consumerism and sells the notion that what you force, wear, or Facebook on honestly defines you. Items are the critical element to happiness and fulfillment.

Many people anticipate social recognition, self-photograph, self esteem and self-esteem development from their purchases. Buying topics for fast non-public gratification is the new black. Overspending our finances, but, can without issues get out of control thinking about the reality that it's so smooth to get credit score score gambling cards nowadays. People with CBD, but, have a greater complicated hassle than "retail treatment."

As I stated earlier than, compulsive looking for serves the brief enhancement of emotional need satisfaction. This emotion-law approach swings among apprehension or tension to a short feeling of frenzy and outstanding excitement at some point of the research and purchase of a few element. This compulsive, vicious shopping for cycle commonly culminates in guilt or regret. When the notion of methods an entire lot cash one spent on commonly useless devices overshadows the powerful clouds, sour remorse falls on them. The regret speedy transforms into tension. And guess in which they grow to be "treating" their tension? Yes, a shop. The circle starts offevolved another time.

The method to the question "Is compulsive looking for a intellectual fitness issue?" is not any. Compulsive spending behavior itself isn't a diagnosable highbrow health scenario. It's more a symptom of various psychological issues, just like the inadequate revel in of self-worth or dependancy. According to 3 researchers, CBD is a shape of obsessive-compulsive contamination. Others consider it some issue much like an impulse manipulate hassle wherein the individual seeks quick-term gratification whilst ignoring prolonged-term effects.

Compulsive spending in maximum times results in compulsive hoarding. People who deliver such brilliant rate to inanimate gadgets have a tendency to sense cumulated pride with the greater they have. Hoarding devices can also provide a fake experience of protection – I'm carefully laid low with this hassle. This leads, however, to three different problem. On the only hand, the greater matters hoarders very personal, the more regular they feel. On the opportunity, the more they've, the greater terrified they come to be of losing it all.

How to Overcome Compulsive Buying

The handiest and fastest manner to triumph over compulsive purchasing for is to raise better emotional awareness. The terrific way is to art work with an authorized therapist. An intention, independent zero.33 birthday party, will let you stay heading in the right direction better than your pals and circle of relatives. Also, a professional will let you with wholesome emotion law strategies to apprehend in which your compulsive purchasing for dispositions come from and triumph over the urge of mindless seeking out within the destiny. The therapist let you pick out out the reasons and horrible consequences of your actions, and help you figure out alternative moves for the compulsive conduct. It is vital to take a look at the tremendous and horrible factors of the compulsive searching out behavior to locate the suitable possibility way of life that satisfies desires while being a lot much less self-negative.

There aren't any precise treatments designed absolutely to triumph over compulsive shopping for behavior, however there are numerous types of therapy that could assist humans address this problem. Two remedy options produce great high-quality consequences: cognitive behavioral remedy, and remedies using one in all a type mindfulness techniques. The former proves to be the first-rate at the same time as applied in agencies. Two psychologists, Michel Lejoyeux and Aviv Weinstein, researched the efficacy of cognitive behavioral treatment in case of CBD. They highlighted that a proper psychiatric assessment want to precede the therapy to discover the maximum appropriate healing software for the affected person. If the affected person receives the most suitable treatment, it's going to decrease their compulsive buying dispositions after only ten weeks of participation. The latter, the mindfulness method, treatments resulted in impulse improvement, better emotion control, and reputation.

People with compulsive buying dispositions may want to likely need to add economic counseling at the side in their psychotherapy. Anything can be beneficial, from self-help books to on-line finance and budgeting publications, to group counseling conferences. Raising monetary consciousness and budgeting development techniques can help loads with going via the financial truth of a person with CBD.

If you feel that you be afflicted via a milder or more immoderate, model of CBD you would possibly need to are searching for advice from a counselor about it. From a budgeting problem of view, it's far crucial to keep your purchasing impulses underneath manipulate. Otherwise, even in case you manipulate to price range and keep inside the short time period, you gained't be capable of maintain it within the lengthy-term.

Chapter 5: Tackling Credit Card Debt

The Most Important Rule

When it involves paying payments (any bill –
now not definitely your credit rating card
bills), it's far important to preserve in
thoughts this: typically pay on time. When
you don't pay your payments on time, many
things can occur:

1. You get charged a late price. The unique
information is (yes, there's right statistics),
depending for your facts with this precise
organization, you could name them up
earlier of time and inform them that you
obtained't be capable of make a price on
time. They might possibly wave the past due
charge for you. Of path, this gained't take
vicinity in case you're frequently past due.

2. Your hobby rate will skip up. Did that
some groups will boom your charge up to
fifteen% after surely one late price? While
you've got them on the telephone, make
certain to invite them approximately your
interest price and if it will growth due to

this. Don't fear about seeking to barter with them each. Sure, you can't slip him a twenty when you shake fingers (I ought to in no way great that flow into), but a touch moral negotiation isn't incorrect. Ethical negotiation = don't auction off your first born.

3. It's a ding on your credit score rating document (even as your price is more than a month past due). It's pretty essential so one can pay your overdue quantity (and costs) as quickly as you could. The longer you wait, the more chance that the business agency will file your overdue price.

four. Your credit score score drops. Did that price facts makes up over a third of your credit rating rating? That's why overdue payments have the type of massive effect for your normal score. Remember that emergency cellphone call that you made to try to avoid that past due price? You also can ask them if this can effect your credit rating rating score. A lot of organizations acquired't report a past due rate proper away (grace durations are first rate and reachable) but don't take their generosity as a proper.

Another Important Rule

Okay, I take that over again. Paying on time is the maximum critical but at a near 2nd is: Pull your loose credit score score file each 365 days to preserve a close to eye on your credit rating. There are a ton of places that offer free versions of your credit rating rating.

Your Credit Card Debt

One of the big approaches an remarkable manner to store money is to cope with your credit score card debt. Once you repay all of those credit score playing playing playing cards, you'll have extra cash to shop or to spend on different requirements anyhow.

Snowball Method

The snowball technique may be traced decrease back to the famous Dave Ramsey, the financial guru. This technique is primarily based on the idea that you want to begin paying off the smallest stability first. Once you pay that off, you pass directly to the following one.

Use the cash that you might have otherwise been the usage of to pay off the smallest account on pinnacle of this everyday rate. After that's paid off, do the equal with the subsequent one. Use the cash that you can have otherwise used on the primary cards to feature on for your regular charge.

Not simplest that, however the snowball method also enables construct your self assurance as you repay your smaller money owed. Because you may see development faster, you revel in higher approximately saving money and paying off your debts. It feels exact to peer that development.

Avalanche Method

This method calls for which you listing off your credit score card (or unique) debts via interest fee. Place the most important hobby charge first and descend from that. Pay off the debt with the first-class interest price first. This makes it so you will pay off your debt quicker and you spend plenty tons much less coins on just clean hobby.

This plan makes loads of enjoy logically, however you need to have some sturdy will-electricity to stick in your plan.

Your Credit Score Is Important.

There are many one in every of a type procedures to lessen to rubble your credit score score rating. Here are 3 big approaches that allows you to reduce to rubble your credit rating score with out even attempting:

1. Use up Your Available Credit.

Yep, there are exquisite strategies to ruin your credit card too – and this is taken into consideration in reality one among them. Don't take their $15,000 credit score score restrict as a project. Your credit score usage ratio (how loads credit score rating score you're certainly using) is pretty influential in identifying what your credit score rating score score is.

So if you have $15,000 of to be had credit score rating and also you burn up $14,999, you can be doing all your credit card and your credit score rating harm. The extremely good ratios are 10% or decrease, but on not unusual, you need to goal for about 30%.

2. Maxing Out More Than One Card

Not most effective is that this a fantastic way to break a credit score score card, but it'll moreover do severa for your credit score score. This ruins your credit score score because it messes together with your credit score score usage ratio – like when you burn up your to be had credit score thru maxing out a card. Just take delivery of as actual with what is going to show up if you max out a couple of of your playing gambling playing cards.

three. Closing Your Highest Limit Card First

Remember credit score score score utilization ratio I cited at number one? Consider this: you've were given a card with a $20,000 limit and one with a $2,000 restrict. Altogether, you've were given $22,000 of available credit score rating. Supposing you've have been given a three,000 dollar stability on the card with the excellent restriction, and $1,000 on the smaller card - that also leaves you with $17,000 of credit rating and a credit score rating usage ratio of about 22%.

Okay, allow's say which you pay off and close to out the card with the wonderful limit. That knocks your to be had credit score score to pleasant $2,000. Your ratio then skyrockets to 50% and your credit rating rating received't like that variety.

Things You Should Know About Credit Cards

Having been within the scenario wherein I didn't recognise what I modified into doing after I first acquired my first credit score rating card, I located that information is one of the fine things you may arm your self with.

1. Having a credit rating rating card doesn't mean that you want to apply it or be in debt.

It isn't black and white. You don't need to hold it locked up or be all of the time in debt. There are first rate techniques of using credit score score gambling playing cards. It is feasible in case you want to apply your credit score card frequently and stay out of debt through charging most effective what you may provide you with the money for to pay at the same time as the bill arrives each month. Of path, to do this, you need to ensure which you preserve a close eye on how masses you're spending.

2. You can without trouble create a reimbursement plan through your self or with the useful useful resource of lenders (although it is probably best not to want to get them involved).

Unlike famous perception, organizations do want you to pay them once more. They don't want you for all time in debt. Creditors and collection groups will artwork with you to extend a compensation plan. You may also even paintings with a credit rating counselor in case you want some advice on arising with a plan that receives you out of the pink but however permits with a purpose to stay a a laugh and healthy life.

three. You can't visit jail for nonpayment, however they're able to take loads from you.

If you have credit rating score card debt and also you don't pay it off, you won't visit prison. However, the businesses can sue you and garnish your wages or belongings because the pick out sees healthy.

four. If you don't pay on time, there are a group of hidden fees to take a look at out for.

Let's say which you close to a credit card account with out in reality looking on the final declaration. That little stability can expand proper into a incredible monster due to past due expenses, interest, and default APR. Not best that, there can be a specific residual hobby that is generated after the invoice is issued and earlier than your charge is obtained. If you may, constantly pay your stability in complete, all of the time. Don't save you making payments after you close up up the account.

five. Don't pass the use of for each credit score rating card to be had.

Having credit score score to be had all the time is good in your credit score score score so the idea stands that if you can get a credit score card, you have to workout for it, proper? Wrong. Every time you comply with for a credit score card, and also you get rejected, it's a ding for your credit score rating rating.

6. Double your be part of up bonus.

Sign up bonuses can be wonderful and they don't usually come round so have your partner or accomplice check for the equal card to double up on those bonuses. Just ensure that you preserve a close to eye on how a bargain you spend. Just due to the truth the ones bonuses are there, doesn't suggest that they may be there all of the time and that you may't overspend.

7. Gift playing cards can be implemented in current approaches too.

If you want to obtain a minimal spending threshold to get a signal-up bonus, use your credit score rating card to buy present playing cards for stores that you go to regularly. You may even use your credit score card to buy coins playing cards. Just make sure which you buy the cards earlier than the reduce-off date. Then you could use the existing gambling cards later. Here's each different trick. If you get bonus factors to your card for getting at high quality locations, like your community grocery shop, purchase your present playing cards there to get the factors, get the sign-up bonus, and feature the winning gambling playing cards to apply later.

Creating Your Budgeting gadget

When budgeting, you are balancing amongst your essential goals, your needs and your monetary desires. Here are the steps on how you can acquire this balance:

Step 1: Identify your financial priorities

The first step calls at the manner to listing all of the topics that you need to your lifestyles that requires a financial dedication. To do that, you need to assume destiny financial dreams.

Identifying future monetary goals

Before you can start a rate variety plan, you want to undergo in thoughts your existence dreams. This isn't always a totally tough

48

project for maximum human beings. We all understand what we need to shop for if we had a few more money. Some people want to tour round the arena for example, at the equal time as others just want to shop for gadgets that supply them comfort in their private houses.

When we speak about dreams in this bankruptcy, but, we are not speaking about patron merchandise or interesting services. We are speaking about critical lifestyles milestones that require coins. Buying a residence, for example, is a profitable goal. Everybody needs his or her personal domestic. The urgency becomes even extra while you're planning to have a own family. You want a home wherein your circle of relatives can expand.

A man or woman with out a notion will now not consider this trouble until it is urgent. A wiser character must count on this destiny need and put together for it financially even as he even though has lots of time. You want to consider your destiny monetary dreams right after this paragraph. You need to list they all down and positioned them so as in line with their importance.

Adding your ardour within the listing

Life might be stupid if we only worked for what we want. The thoughts desires a bit pride now after which. If we count on existence is interesting, we're extra prompted to artwork.

This is wherein your passions are available. Aside out of your desires, you furthermore can also want to offer finances on your passions. If you adore visiting, you may despite the fact that do it even if you are following a price range, as long as it's far planned and your profits justifies such trips.

You want to take this time to think about the few luxuries that you could allow your self and your family to enjoy. You need to have the assignment not to overdo the ones luxuries. You need to most effective do them to re-encourage your self and the opportunity contributors of your own family to hold saving.

Step 2: Set the proper amount of cash for your need and desires

Now that you understand what you want to buy, you want to make a monthly expenses listing. When making your listing, you need to divide all of your charges into classes. Here are some of the commonplace price lessons:

- Food

- Utility bills

- Transportation prices

- Toiletries, laundry and special home protection charges

These are the prices commonplace to all adults. Some humans, but, produce other price lessons of their lives. Here are a few examples:

- Kids' desires

- Sports and fitness

- Pets

In some months, you can additionally want to invest in more crucial subjects. If you have got a modern manner, for example, you could want new clothes so as to make you wholesome in. If this is the case, you could need to include a garments rate variety for that month. For the holidays, you will additionally want to include affords and tour meals instructions. By together with those seasonal costs, you will be prepared financially for all of them.

You ought to additionally make precise categories for precise types of fees that you choice to keep tune of. If you're responsible of spending too much on eating out, as an example, you may want to reduce in this class. However, we usually encompass this magnificence with food fees. To maintain track of your ordinary ingesting-out costs, you need to make a unique class for it and separate it from the meals class.

After list all your charge instructions, you need to recognize how lots cash each category desires each month. The amount that you want to set apart for meals, for instance, relies upon at the form of people for your circle of relatives. You want to set regular amounts for those instructions.

You must additionally count on the quantity which you need to spend on training that do not have a hard and rapid price. Your strength bill, as an instance, varies each month. You want to put together for the americaand downs of those styles of prices.

Employing a budgeting rule

Aside from the techniques noted above, you may additionally exercise a budgeting rule to make sure which you do now not overspend every month. Here are a number of them:

eighty-10-10 Rule

The 80-10-10 rule is the proper one to study. This rule generally approach that you spend eighty% of your internet income to your want and dreams. 10% of your income need to visit charity on the equal time because the closing 10% need to go to your monetary financial savings. The rule lets in you to share your earnings along side your network at the same time as notwithstanding the fact that saving to your prolonged-term goals.

60-10-30 Rule

This rule is stricter than the simplest above. You can use it if you can live really with 60% of your internet profits. 10% still goes to charity, and the 30% goes in your economic monetary savings. By saving a bigger part of your earnings, you'll be able to gain your economic dreams faster.

50% Rule

You need to use this rule when you have money owed to pay or whilst there may be an pressing brief-term motive that you need to attain. In this budgeting rule, you attempt to make all your want and desires in form with simplest 50% of your net profits. The distinctive 50% is allocated to your savings. If your need and goals notwithstanding the reality that move beyond your 50% of your earnings, you want to reduce on some masses a good deal less important price lessons.

Step three: Adjust your way of existence and dreams regular collectively together with your income diploma

At this thing, you apprehend about the topics that you want to spend on proper now and the future financial commitments which you need to keep for. By now, you need to already comprehend in case your monthly income may additionally can help you fund your lifestyle and save on your future financial dreams.

If you're one of the lucky ones, there can be a few extra cash left in the end your charges and monetary savings. For most humans, but, the earnings they bring approximately approximately in will not be sufficient to fund their contemporary way of existence and hold for massive goals on the identical time. If you have the same experience, you have to bear in mind readjusting a few areas of your existence.

You ought to first check some of the types which you indexed above and the corresponding quantity allotted for those rate variety. You need to pick out out areas wherein you could reduce returned so that you ought to have extra money for financial savings.

Increase your earnings

If your profits is low, no quantity of cutbacks will let you hold. If you continue to can not store after excessive cutbacks in all your spending classes, you need to find out opportunities as a manner to boom your profits. If your desires require a big sum of money and you high-quality have a short duration to shop for it, you furthermore mght want to take this approach.

Step 4: Allocate your cash as quick as you get preserve of it

When your earnings arrives, the primary element that you need to do is to distribute them properly. The first allocation ought to visit your financial savings. By putting cash apart as speedy as you got them, you'll now not be tempted to spend too much on groceries or buying.

The next classes that you need to allocate for are your important wishes, crucial software payments, and other crucial bills. You should not forget about these areas due to the truth it is very inconvenient in case you pass over those bills.

The subsequent vicinity which you want to allocate for is your easy needs. You need to set cash aside for food and groceries.

The amount left should be allocated to all of the different important charges which you have indexed. If there may be though a few left after allocating your coins, you can spend a few part of it in your entertainment or your passions. You also can allocate the cash for next month's charges.

If you get keep of extra quantities, you've got a preference to feature it in your savings or to spend it for topics and opinions that bring quick-time period happiness. We propose that you preserve it for your dreams. The extra money you shop, the faster you can obtain your monetary dreams.

Step 5: Track your money

As said within the preceding chapters, you need to be aware of wherein your cash is going. Money flows interior and from your price range fund. You must ensure that more money is going in than out. To be capable of apprehend wherein your coins is going, you need to be aware of in which each penny is going.

By tracking your cash, you'll be able to ensure which you are following your deliberate price range. If you study which you are spending too fast within the meals class, for instance, you may take measures which will allow you to keep your food charges low.

To be able to tune your coins resultseasily, you want a tool which you are familiar with. Here are some of the commonplace gear used by expert budgeters:

1. Notebook and ledger

The only device to apply is a pocket ebook that permits you to characteristic a logbook wherein you location all your fees for the day. It desires to be small enough that you can convey spherical. Before the day ends, you want to switch your records to a larger ledger. You can searching for advice from your ledger to analyze your spending behavior.

2. Smartphone app

If you're a smartphone man or woman, there are loose apps a very good manner to will can help you update the pocket e-book device. Every time you spend, you can truly perform your cellular telephone and listing your prices. You need to make this activity a dependancy each time you spend. This is a better possibility than a pocket ebook due to the fact we bring our cellular phone everywhere we glide. Unlike the pocket ebook, the app does not grow to be full with out hassle. If it will become whole, you only want to uninstall the app and reinstall it to wipe records away.

There are top price apps to be had that offer those types of services, but in case you do now not have the price range, there also are unfastened apps that offer limited capabilities. For maximum people, the competencies of the loose apps are enough to keep a every day, weekly and monthly report of their prices.

3. Spreadsheet

Instead of a ledger, you must use a spreadsheet record to maintain all your price statistics. If you are familiar with the use of this sort of tool, you will be capable of make calculations quicker and make fast interpretations of records provided.

You can use Numbers for Mac or Microsoft Excel if you have those programs in your laptop. If no longer, you may moreover use open source options available for download on-line. The open supply alternatives' functions are enough for this reason.

Tips on tracking your prices:

• Keep track of even the smallest charges

People who're new to monitoring their cash typically have a tendency to forget about about the small prices. You want to keep in mind that every one the small fees add up. Over the route of 6 months or a year, the ones small fees will upload as an awful lot as a big quantity.

• Keep your monitoring descriptions accurate

When checking your expenses in, you need to offer all your notes with correct descriptions. If you're making vague descriptions, you could no longer consider where the charge changed into made, and you can now not be capable of categorize the costs nicely.

• Keep receipts or notes while you don't have your tracking device

There are instances whilst your monitoring gear aren't available. Your cellphone can be useless, or your pocket e-book can be complete. That is why you have to typically ask for a receipt for all of your purchases. If a receipt is not available, you have to ask for a piece of paper from the payee so that you may additionally need to make a phrase of all of your costs. You have to area those notes to your pockets and skip once more to them on the prevent of the day.

• Check your prices document each 12 hours

In the begin, it is going to be difficult on the way to be aware of all of your costs. You may additionally pass over a few costs when you are in a rush. To save you lapses in recording your costs, you should set your alarm for 12 hours. When the alarm goes off, you need to set apart some element you're doing and test if your spending information are complete. You will comprehend in case you not noted taking note of a few charges if there may be a discrepancy amongst your statistics and the cash left to your wallet.

Chapter 6: Why Do You Need A Budget?

We also can have misconceptions about the rich and the way they spend their cash. We are often supplied with images of rich people calmly using their coins on a couple of cars or expensive clothes they'll located on perhaps as soon as. However, the ones are usually the lifestyles of the extraordinarily wealthy and don't reflect the lives of the human beings who've owned corporations, and diligently worked those operations till they were financially solid. We may also moreover envy the über wealthy for his or her spending competencies, however being financially free doesn't should be that superficial or perhaps that an extended manner past our very private values and way.

To Secure Money for Your Needs and Most Important Expenses

If you've ever heard of Maslow's hierarchy of desires, then you definitely really recognize there's a piece of an order with which you want to prioritize your dreams (McLeod, 2020). First, there are fundamental survival desires: You've were given to feed and get dressed your self; you want an area to stay and sleep. Then, you've have been given to ensure you experience steady in that place, in addition to inside your manner. That is, are you confident for your very own functionality to hold your source of income and resources? If you don't revel in a experience of safety in how you offer for your self and for your family, it's going to be very hard to transport onto prioritizing wishes like relationships and simple fitness and properly-being, now not to say self-achievement and reason.

In remarkable phrases, in case you're continuously worried about making ends meet, you'll be too harassed to try to "get ahead" financially. Your thoughts can be constantly placing out the fires of paying bills earlier than their due dates or before they reduce off the lighting. Setting the muse of monetary independence isn't feasible if all you're doing is spending your assets, strive, and time playing whack-a-mole together with your financial obligations.

Budgeting is about getting easy on what your real goals are—what you want for survival—and scoping out a clean plan for a way you'll meet the ones needs month after month with out worry. When you recognize you're now not going to want to embarrass your self on the prevent of the month with the useful resource of inquiring for but some other extension in your rent, your mind is unfastened to worry about different subjects. When you're regular, you're much more likely to be more assured financially, and this will reason a bit extra optimism and wiggle room for what you could do in conjunction with your cash. This is the start of allowing your self to enhance your existence, as opposed to virtually trying to make it to the following paycheck.

To Improve Your Relationship With Money with the useful resource of the use of Seeing Your Bad Habits More Clearly

Taking a take a look at your horrible conduct with cash isn't always any stroll within the park. You're no longer truly losing a slight on what's been retaining you all over again. You're going to be focused on and magnifying your manner of considering and behaving within the direction of money. This says hundreds about who you are as someone, and getting a high-quality observe ourselves within the replicate isn't a venture for the faint of coronary heart. No doubt budgeting is difficult if you're no longer familiar with doing it, especially within the beginning. While a budget is a smooth roadmap, it's no longer an clean mission to get ourselves grew to come to be round and on course if we've been running hard, handiest to find out we've been going inside the wrong path this complete time! You would probably need to double yet again, you may need to undergo the equal web site traffic another time, or you may in all likelihood even need to pay greater toll costs, however you need to determine that going thru the trouble of finding out your plan is properly nicely well well worth it in case you don't want to grow to be West when you certainly supposed to transport East.

Looking at how massive of a hole you've dug your self in financially can be embarrassing and disheartening, however you don't climb out of that hole via mindlessly digging deeper. Be inclined to have a look at what you've were given thus far. If subjects are a massive wide variety, then determine that you'll smooth it out no matter what. If you've ever finished a spring cleaning of your home, then you recognize matters commonly get mainly worse in advance than any semblance of order starts offevolved to appear. Be willing to test the mess—it's far yours ultimately, and that is your threat to easy it up.

To Bookmark Money for Future Goals

Have you ever heard of the marshmallow take a look at? This emerge as a take a look at in behind schedule gratification carried out with youngsters and treats. The youngsters were given a address, but confident that in the event that they waited 15 mins with out consuming it, they might be rewarded with a similarly cope with. When the study checked in on those children years down the road into their maturity, the check confirmed that those youngsters who had been capable of flow 15 minutes expecting the second one cope with showed extra success financially, of their careers, and loads of various regions of their lives than the youngsters who didn't wait the least bit (Mischel & Ebbesen, 1970).

What's the issue of you expertise this tale? The kids who waited were gambling the prolonged-term sport. They have been willing to attend and maintain off on gratification now, if it supposed gaining more in a while. Just like the ones kids who want to eat their veggies to expand up large and sturdy, you want to begin a price range if you need the chance to live the life you've always dreamt about. That being stated, what does your dream existence look like? Remember the want for that clear excursion spot. Not excellent will you be capable of get again at the proper tune faster even as you comprehend in which you're going, you're moreover more likely to stay the course if you're excited to get there.

To Reduce Any Overspending and Achieve Debt Freedom More Quickly

This one is going without announcing, but we frequently may not recognize we're overspending until we've gotten a robust test our budget and characteristic a smooth idea of what our options are. Once you check your costs, it could display to you a few areas in that you lack know-how. Could this be a chance to save coins, or at least get greater fee to your dollar? Many human beings don't usually comprehend in which they're overspending, and don't start asking questions or seeking out fees till a easy price variety is performed.

You'll moreover be able to better gauge if you could genuinely provide you with the coins for a few thing or now not. Maybe shopping for a emblem-new car isn't the first rate idea, if you can't have sufficient cash the right coverage or safety expenses that go together with it. When you located everything collectively into one spreadsheet or document, there's a whole lot less of a threat of you forgetting approximately nice costs or getting caught with the aid of wonder with emergencies. This approach you may offer an give up date in your debt! You'll ultimately have an concept of on the identical time as you'll get out of debt, although it's simplest a ballpark. Doing away with horrible behavior turns into lots simpler definitely because of the truth you have got a clear date and an exciting aim in mind. This by myself is motivation enough for installing area better conduct with your coins.

To Manage Every Financial Decision and Prepare for Challenges

We already realize that existence has its the united states of americaand downs, but being able to meet your want and desires shouldn't be a guessing interest. One of the strategies to help mitigate the outcomes of a economic dry spell is to don't forget that it's now not going to very last all the time. There may be a time while you'll all all over again find out your self once more on strong ground. The next time you do, but, you want to remind your self of the manner stressful and tough your last dry spell modified into. The key isn't to strive to interrupt out them, however to prepare for them. Whenever you find your self feasting, don't gorge yourself; set a few provisions apart for those instances your home may not be so bountiful.

We're often chastised to be continuously grinding and disciplining ourselves—all paintings and no play—but without a doubt the answer lies someplace inside the middle. While you ought to take benefit of a brilliant harvest and maintain up all you could, you may additionally give you the cash for to enjoy some of those gadgets now. Life doesn't need to be a consistent swing among dinner party and famine. If you find out your stability with dealing with cash, you'll constantly be capable of consume well regardless of the season.

The key to economic independence is being proactive in preference to reactive. Those who set the fashion as opposed to take a look at are commonly those who take gain of its fulfillment.

To Live Within Your Means and Put Money to Work for You in a Positive Way

Once you've gotten a clean photograph of genuinely wherein you stand financially, you may be pleasantly surprised to apprehend that there's extra you're capable of do in conjunction with your money than you idea. If you're like maximum of the Americans within the CNBC data being trampled through own family debt, however, it is able to come as a surprise to comprehend that your manner aren't as splendid as you as quickly as concept (Fay, 2021). While you shouldn't surrender yourself to little technique for the rest of your days, that is the wakeup call you want to really test your lifestyles and the manner you've been living it to this point. A huge part of the blame may be laid on the fingers of advertising and marketing classified ads and Hollywood's depiction of the not unusual circle of relatives. Both spouses may be strolling jobs with common salaries, but one way or the opposite control to live in an better-beauty community with present day vehicles inside the storage and each teen signed up for a recreation or a few form of musical lesson. The focus of the show might be the wit of the script and the passion of the characters, however we because the target audience can't help however subtly assume, "This is the manner of life of the common American." As lengthy as the budget aren't a part of the plot, Hollywood may also or won't screen the struggles at preserving the sort of lifestyle on a mean profits.

While residing underneath our manner in no manner sounds a laugh and will often without a doubt sound defeating, it is an possibility to take a better test your way. Sheryl Crow's lyrics from Soak up the Sun come to thoughts: "It's no longer having what you want/It's attempting what you've have been given" (2002). This concept may additionally moreover appear trite, in particular in case you is probably suffering with some factor like debt, however behaviors and conduct are regularly modified with a chunk of a perspective shift. Instead of living beneath your method, how approximately seeing it as living in a manner that protects your future and that of your circle of relatives's?

What Does a Budget Look Like?

If budgeting isn't honestly as awful as we regularly make it out to appear, then what does it absolutely seem like? Can it additionally be a pleasant revel in? Before you roll your eyes at the idea of a laugh and budget worked into the identical sentence, test what includes a finances. Here's a touch: You're not intended to take a look at its suggestions; it's imagined to fit you—your desires for cash and your thoughts-set spherical wealth.

The Basic Components of Every Kind of Budget

A finances, without a doubt placed, is ready studying cash coming in and going out. While there's no unmarried right manner of creating organized and using a price variety, as we'll see inside the next phase; there are primary additives to how a rate range works.

You have to first take stock of your earnings, of direction, however make certain to expose all resources of income. We can frequently overlook approximately about such things as authorities subsidies or tax credit rating, but if it's coins you're going to spend, then it counts as income. Were it no longer coming in, must you've got had been given provided the ones extra materials in your industrial organization or gotten the youngsters those new shoes all of them needed? Don't take any variables as a right, mainly on the begin of drawing up a budgeted sport plan. We frequently don't recognize in reality how hundreds we will certainly have enough money or not find out the cash for till we've were given it down on paper.

Also, have in mind of your tax bracket. You may additionally need to document your income in its net form, however be careful of your gross income as well because of the fact this could element in at tax time. Will you have saved sufficient cash all through the 12 months so one can with out problem and right now pay over again what you owe, or will you warfare for the relaxation of the 365 days with a central authority charge plan? Likewise, the equal diligence have to be applied while you acquire a tax pass decrease lower back from the government. Will you spend your newfound wealth, or will you intentionally positioned it toward the goals on your task plan, bringing you that a whole lot towards your freedom? When calculating correct projections of your income, it is probably a outstanding idea to lean towards downplaying the ones projections. You want to be prepared and capable of meet your costs and different desires even at some point of your slowest and lowest months of earnings.

Fixed charges are normally the ideal to cope with due to the fact you could charge variety them without hassle right proper right into a plan. You apprehend you'll constantly want to pay them month after month at the same charge. One problem to keep in mind, but, is looking at them another time on a each year basis, because of the fact you will possibly want to recollect such things as inflation, upgrades, or downgrades.

Variable expenses are next, and they're handiest a tad bit trickier. They're figures that don't exchange overly a whole lot, but you may find yourself ballparking a monthly allowance for them an exquisite manner to keep up with bills. Your heating bill, for example, may also moreover furthermore come each place in location of on a monthly basis, and based totally for your utilization in that point, the charge will variety from area to place. That being stated, you'd ought to calculate your commonplace month-to-month payments, ideally based virtually at the months in which your utilization have turn out to be the notable. This manner, you may set a small quantity aside precise for the heating bill each month, in preference to scrambling to find out 3 months' absolutely nicely well worth of fees to pay at the same time as the time comes. We'll flow into detail later about the way to bypass about doing this. For now, it's enough to apprehend how variable charges paintings, and why it's exceptional to maintain them in a separate class for your regular fees.

Then, you'd need to preserve a record of any discretionary costs. These are basically charges which may be terrific and no longer essential to the going for walks of your circle of relatives. Think of your goals rather than your goals—eating out or any leisure sports

sports can be considered discretionary, as an example. With all subjects regarding your expenses' projections, you can want to do the alternative of what you did collectively together with your income. That is, in location of downplaying your month-to-month expenses, overestimate what they might be at the manner to offer your self a piece of a cushion if your expenses without a doubt do become better than expected.

The final item each form of rate variety ought to detail in is goals! Don't overlook the ones—notwithstanding them being final in your list and the least pressing out of all of your finances objects, they're the complete purpose for beginning your price variety in the first place. We'll skip into element approximately the proper developments surrounding goal setting and mentality a chunk later. For now, without a doubt undergo in thoughts on the spot dreams you're currently strolling with, further to desires which you'd need to reap inside the next three to 5 years, and then past.

We'll quick cross into the data of each budgeting thing we've mentioned to this point and help you to create a step-with the beneficial aid of-step project plan as a manner to start the device as painlessly as feasible. Make brilliant to take each class into consideration, and don't be afraid to have too many. As you keep to make use of your price range and confirm your plan, you'll cultivate a machine and approach that's proper for you. That being stated, with every sort of fee variety, it's vital to study, assume once more, and re-engage month after month till you got your dreams.

There's No One Way to Budget

Whether making a decision to hold your charge range in a pocket book, or on a spreadsheet on the Cloud, or making a decision to down load a budgeting app to your cellphone or tool completely is based totally upon on you. Many humans use an app because of ease of use, but others use their pocket ebook for the very same cause. Which one is best for you? Furthermore, we generally recall aesthetic reasons for the use of a budgeting device as having little to no priority, however if some thing is visually proper to you, you may locate it much less tough to open it up, otherwise you'll actually apprehend it extra. Something that's too chaotic or complicated-searching might in all likelihood dissuade you from sticking to the plan. Looking at your budgeting information must give you a clean standard image of what's taking location with you financially, however notwithstanding the fact that be concise enough that will help you apprehend the records of your plan. In exclusive phrases, in case you turn out to be pressured virtually with the resource of looking at the finances sheet, then you definitely definately may additionally need to rethink your display.

Make those entire lists and instructions keeping in thoughts that this project is like growing a roadmap or recipe. Where are you looking to circulate, or what are you trying to make? Also do not forget what it takes to get to that holiday spot, or to make that recipe. When using a GPS, do you want the audio on or off? Do you have to keep it excessive at the dashboard, or actually have a examine it every few miles or so? Let's use the cooking recipe metaphor. Do you have a small kitchen, or is it large? Do you have got got an array of kitchen domestic gadget and system to bake and cook dinner dinner with, or are you strolling with one mixing bowl and a spatula? Do you be aware how it's no longer definitely about having a GPS or a recipe? How you use these tools topics. It's going to determine performance and ease of use, and on the way to in flip inspire you to use the gadget you have got very well and continuously. Quality and consistency then determine success. Therefore, it's crucial to be privy to what works for you and what doesn't month after month. If you locate you're struggling with using your rate range sheet, remember the fact which you might not be the hassle! The manner in which you use your gear can be deterring you from fulfillment. In the ones first few months, be aware of what you want approximately your charge range and what you don't; what allows make clear the bigger photograph of your dreams and what in fact confuses you. Adjust your charge variety therefore. The extra you align your charge variety for your conduct and behaviors, the much more likely you are to enhance the beneficial ones and replace the bad ones.

Leave Nothing Out

One final examine on what goes into a fee range is to leave not some thing out. You may additionally moreover have already stuck that drift, but it bears repeating. Everything desires to show up in your plan if you want to make this system as capacity as feasible. Things that aren't expected usually supply your budgeting plan an Achilles' heel. Of path, there'll continuously be surprising fees or emergencies that require cash, but we already apprehend that existence has its united statesand downs. We'll talk a chunk later about developing an emergency fund, and why it's so essential to surely preserve it for a moist day.

As backwards as it is able to sound, block out time to your time desk and price range for the sudden. That is to say, anticipate to be thrown off path now and then. The intention of a fee variety isn't to conform with the blueprints flawlessly. The goal is to be prepared for the sudden and prepared to move all over again to the drawing board time and again.

Before You Start Your Budget

Decide Why You Want to Begin Budgeting Your Money

Deciding why you need to start budgeting isn't as obvious as it can sound. "I must simply have a price range for myself," or "Budgeting is a really wonderful concept," aren't reasons enough for getting started out. This is genuinely because of the fact there's no actual purpose or purpose connected to this reasoning. Just because of the reality we 'want to' do some factor does not compel us to truely get started out. We understand we must devour nicely. We recognize we need to in reality employ that health club club by way of way of way of starting again up on Monday. Does this sort of self-speak ever in reality encourage us to do any of those topics? This form of questioning clearly makes budgeting sound like a punishment, and if we by no means get round to it, we experience like we're being 'horrible.' Knowing why you're doing something now not nice creates interest and motivation, but it furthermore creates enthusiasm for the everyday obligations that flow into sporting out a plan. Your motives don't should be grand or fancy. They in reality want to be yours and deeply vast to you.

Prioritize Your Goals via way of way of Level of Importance

When listing some of your goals, fee them on a scale of 1 to ten. You may want to possibly need to have every intention require rankings: One thinking about urgency, and the second one rating considering significance. Just due to the fact some element is pressing doesn't make it essential. The electric powered powered invoice that's due subsequent week is urgent and critical within the revel in which you want to keep the lighting on, but it's now not part of the list of dreams that comprise your dreams. What kind of emotion is connected to the desires you have got had been given? This is a remarkable manner of figuring out how critical a few element is to you.

Additionally, be cautious of the kinds of goals you place, and the intensity with that you set them. We've thus far checked out budgeting through the lens of dread and overwhelm, however you may very well enjoy a enjoy of empowerment on the concept of getting your financial affairs at the right song. That being said, be careful now not to certainly overhaul your whole lifestyles with goals. If you get carried away too rapid, you hazard getting crushed after which giving up. The way to without a doubt cement exchange is with the useful resource of beginning out little by little, preferably one goal at a time. Perhaps, start off with one brief-term motive (inside the subsequent six months), one medium-term purpose (in the subsequent 3 to five years), and one prolonged-time period intention (5 years or longer).

Set a Time Limit for Your Goals

With the ones 3 excellent kinds of dreams, you'll be aware the timeline, and that's critical. A remaining date may additionally moreover provide you with a revel in of urgency, and that experience can also make the reason extra real. Imagine living out your short-time period cause six months from now. Pick a actual date and positioned it on your planner or calendar. We all realize how rapid six months will pass. It also gives you a chunk of shape, due to the fact you'll be higher capable of decide what wants to get finished within the subsequent six months to hit your short-term goal.

Having a remaining date can also make clean how a whole lot sincerely desires to get done. Did you want to place a widespread amount aside for a down charge on a residence interior years? If you've got a reason of putting $20,000 apart within the next years, then you definately truly'd need to have a take a look at saving about $835 a month. When you have got a have a examine it this manner, are you succesful of truly workout that quantity of cash to your rate range right now, or will you want to push your dream of a home in advance multiple more years?

List the Things You Want or Enjoy and How Much They Cost

Remember that discretionary fund? It can also, luckily or sadly, be time to rein it in. Creating a rate variety for fun stuff can also experience such as you're placing tips on actually playing your self and your life now. However, expertise that there's a sure sum of money you could spend on a few element you'd like this month at the same time as nevertheless being financially responsible and securing your future, will make spending that fun money more fun. It may not appear like that earlier than the whole lot, however while you understand what sum of money is in fact being wasted or overindulged after doing all of your price range, you'll enjoy extra assured to your very personal ability to paste to your plan. This is certainly in which you find out in which your awful behavior and behaviors lie, and you could greater with out difficulty root them out.

Be Willing to Let Go

What are you inclined to allow circulate of? You also can discover that there are a first rate many things that you can outcomes allow circulate of if you find a number of waste and overindulgence on your spending behavior. However, allow's move a step similarly. Are there devices in your price range that you can let pass of clearly or for a few months at a time? Does your family make a addiction of going to the movies? Can you guys determine as a unit to forego the films for the following six months and feature a circle of relatives sport night time time time or Netflix your favorite films as an alternative? Can you decide to going for walks out at domestic, or downgrading your club at the gym? These are small techniques you could save cash even as although getting what you need. The extra you finances, the more you realise that you may no matter the truth that experience your existence even though it is on much less.

Identify Your Weak Areas and Brainstorm Solutions

Now which you have a higher idea of your lousy behavior and plenty much less-than-favorable behaviors, can you brainstorm a manner to artwork via or round them to enlarge higher ones? Now which you're making plans, do you understand how a bargain you spend on food? It may be an top notch time to get your health behavior in test in addition on your financial behavior. You can in reality begin to supply lunch to paintings as opposed to heading to the mall's cafeteria each day. Do you store at the same time as you're harassed? This may be an exquisite time to research the connection between your cash and your concerns. While coping with stress and anxiety is past the scope of this ebook, searching at your cash problems can start to shed slight on specific areas of your lifestyles that you warfare with. The manner you cope with your coins is the manner you spot your self. So it can be useful to look at your charge variety from the attitude of workout your issue and improving your outlook on life, now not just on squeezing out coins wherein you could.

Gather Your Financial Documents (All of Them!)

This can be the most stressful part of building a finances, however it'll be beneficial to you to collect up all the economic documents which may be applicable and modern-day-day for your profits and costs. Going thru the lot may be as revealing as in truth list out how a whole lot you spend and wherein. Once we buy a life coverage coverage or create an investment portfolio at the financial institution, we have a propensity to record the ones office work away right right into a cabinet inside the domestic administrative center that we by no means open up again. In having them reemerge, you can apprehend that the economic merchandise you idea you had aren't exactly what you need. You might also comprehend that you're not getting as an lousy lot cost for the fee you're spending, or that what you're saving is in reality now not sufficient for the lengthy-term.

Without each issue of your price range in the budget, the plan need to with out problems fall apart, making you need to give up or obliging you to spend even more time reorganizing everything. Mistakes do seem inside the starting and subjects do land up forgotten, but don't in reality take an object as a right truely as it might be a small amount of money paid one time. The dollars upload up as you'll see, and each bit will make a contribution to each your benefit or your detriment. You don't need to wait till it's too past because of find out which it's going to likely be.

Chapter 7: How To Build A Budget

Let's get into the data of what every fee range want to have and the way you should begin breaking down every detail. The information on this bankruptcy can be used for any sort of budgeting device you select to customize for yourself. These are the fundamentals of building a budgeting gadget little by little.

Step 1: Determine Your Income

This is wherein every charge variety starts offevolved offevolved, of course, but you shouldn't take as a right the truth that you could apprehend your month-to-month profits off the pinnacle of your head. It's well well worth studying and noting down wherein each greenback comes from and at the same time as you may count on them to are available in each month.

Remember the little rule approximately the use of your internet profits? What you may take home is what you'll be budgeting, however you do need to maintain in thoughts what you're being taxed from your gross earnings. If you count on to pay a few taxes again at the give up of the yr, then it is probably properly worth the greater try of sitting down along facet your accountant to determine how tons you could want to squirrel away each month as a manner to lessen the blow come tax-time. On the opposite hand, if you normally have a tendency to get a tax cross returned on the prevent of the 12 months, it'd be encouraged to now not aspect that into your annual profits definitely but. It is regularly "out of sight, out of mind" close to your tax return, because of the reality then you acquired't be relying on it to tide you over. It'd be an unpleasant surprise to understand you're not getting as lots as you notion or now not something the least bit if that have been the case. Consider your tax pass decrease again as a bit gift. After you've filed your taxes, and what you're getting again, you could relaxation confident which you've achieved sufficient budgeting through using then to realise precisely in that you'd like to use that more. So, assign a motive to the ones extra tax dollars in advance than they'll be definitely deposited into your account. You'd be performing proactively and correctly, in order that no dollar is wasted or lost.

Also, remember to encompass all varieties of earnings like we mentioned earlier than, which incorporates alimony or little one assist, any interest or dividends you are making on any of your investments, and any rental earnings you can earn. Don't forget to price variety your abnormal or variable profits at its lowest months, so that you're normally prepared to take care of yourself even sooner or later of a slow season. Furthermore, any months wherein your variable income is better is a plus! Mind you, it's critical to plot beforehand for the ones immoderate seasons as a way to take complete gain of that spending functionality. If you pick out to splurge, splurge nicely, however don't always let or now not it's miles impulsive, in any other case you run the chance of feeling guilty in a while. This does not some thing to your attitude and your self-discipline to maintain regular with the rate range. With all matters that should do with budgeting your earnings, whether or now not it's steady or variable, stay as flexible and as open to exchange as you can, especially on the outset of your new budgeting behavior. The beginning is virtually in which those behavior get installation. Be more careful to hold on top of the whole thing so as to deliver yourself the remarkable shot of executing your plans powerfully.

Step 2: Calculate Your Expenses

In this section, we'll get into the remarkable print of your costs. You got a bit of an overarching view in the final economic spoil, but we'll take aside every of the number one classes so you can determine the way you'd like to start growing your personal lists and lessons.

First Determine What's Essential and What's Nonessential

Creating separate lists of requirements instead of nonessentials will be an effective manner to begin. Items like your own home, food, and possibly transportation glide to your first list without query, even as the nonessential gadgets to your 2nd listing can be positioned away inside the interim. Until you decide what's maximum pressing on your dreams and what form of they value, your nonessentials must stay negotiable. Keep an open thoughts!

A useful undertaking is probably to transport again a year and survey your economic group statements and coins receipts, or even your credit score score rating card statements—in case you war with debt, then mainly your credit score rating score card statements. Tracking down the entirety that turn out to be an price to you is a daunting assignment, positive, however preserve in thoughts which you'll only need to do that multiple times within the starting. Take that weekend you promised your self to type via everything. Having saved this promise will on my own make you a chunk extra confident in your self and your scenario.

Likewise, you may likely come upon a bunch of prices which you completely forgot approximately or unnoticed. Look once more at those forgotten gadgets and assume to your self in the event that they were clearly without a doubt well worth the cash spent. If you forgot about them, chances are they didn't supply masses fee into your existence. This is a first rate signal that those fall into your nonessential magnificence.

Fixed vs Variable

Having set the nonessential list aside, observe your necessities and decide which charges are fixed. They are the very great to start with because they're the same each month. Do be aware, however, (probable via way of setting a celeb subsequent to them) which gadgets may be suffering from inflation next year. This little heads-up will higher put together you at 12 months's prevent, mitigating any opportunities of surprise and sadness. Chances are these are feelings you've been experiencing for far too prolonged as regards to your charge variety.

When it includes variable fees, calculate them the identical manner you may your variable income, tremendous this time it might be beneficial to calculate the months wherein the costs charge the best. Whether or not this factors in properly together

together along with your profits, you'd should see for your self, but the idea is that you may meet your goals whilst the charge of them is at their maximum, regardless of the fact that your earnings is at its lowest.

Listing Each of Your Expenditures in Their Various Categories

Some human beings truely lump each of their bills into instructions like utilities, groceries, and so forth. Some others make an effort to list out each item and their respective fees in sub-training. There's no incorrect way of making your lists; the solution is some issue makes you cushty and powerful. As a newbie, you could need to start off list each and every really considered one of your devices because it'll offer you with a bit extra flexibility and let you see exactly wherein your spending is going, so that you can regulate brief with out too many hitches.

The following is a listing of the various sorts of costs you can incur whether regular or variable, vital or nonessential. You're probably already properly aware about those due to the fact you're living out the ones charges every day, however it'll offer you with a brief photograph of what there's to undergo in thoughts and to look out for.

Housing—This, of direction, is your rent or loan, but don't neglect devices like belongings taxes or insurances. Think through any sorts of costs you would in all likelihood have in terms of your property as nicely. Those have a propensity to sneak up on you.

Utilities—These are charges like your heating or fuel bill, however moreover your mobile cellphone or safety device. If you're renting, your landlord may moreover have been so kind as to encompass a number of these items into your lease already. In that case, keep in mind no longer each assets proprietor may additionally do this with variable charges like heating or fuel, and your personal landlord may additionally very well alternate up the pay structure in the future. You don't continually have to apprehend those fees if they'll be covered in your lease, however do preserve in thoughts they may be there. You use them on your everyday life, so it's important to endure your use of them in thoughts.

Household devices—Any expenses that bypass into preserving or keeping a own family fall underneath this category. This includes such things as gardening and landscaping prices, or ornament or safety prices too.

Groceries—Factor in first-rate the meals you purchase for your circle of relatives on a normal basis, and we'll communicate about eating out in simplest a 2d. Besides meals, but, embody items which you may also purchase along aspect your meals at the grocery preserve. These are objects like cleaning merchandise and sources, or toiletries. You buy those on a normal basis, however likely not as often due to the fact the meals.

Living charges—Besides your family objects and groceries, the ones can embody the property you buy on your pets, when you have any. Although, they can also embody gadgets like normal banking prices! Don't take those as a proper, despite the fact that the charges are minimal and also you don't be aware them coming out every month. They devour away (albeit, very slowly) at something profits goes into those money owed.

Transportation—Consider no longer virtually automobile bills or your bus bypass, but items like fuel, parking expenses, and coverage charges too.

Health—Life or incapacity insurances fall underneath this magnificence, similarly to any costs in the direction of drug remedies and so on. This one might be more hard to do not forget in case you don't have any insurance and pay out of pocket for any dental appointments or emergencies. For that, you could test probable the remaining five years truly well well worth of health costs. Likewise, preserve in mind any plans you can must restore your enamel or dispose of understanding teeth and such. How approximately blood exams? Your pleasure and lengthy existence must be motivation enough to want to decorate your fitness, but you could need to endure in thoughts the reality that preventative measures for staying wholesome are less costly through the years than had been you to miss your health, after which need to deal with a superb infection setback in some time. Take care of your self for the sake of your fitness and your pockets.

Personal charges—Any costs towards smoking or alcohol may not always fall underneath the grocery magnificence if you don't purchase them frequently sufficient. You may additionally need to furthermore recollect any income spent on music, audiobooks, normal books, and so forth.

Eating out—Keep any cash spent on eating place dinners or consuming out for lunch in a separate class for your expenses on food. You want to distinguish amongst what's crucial and what certainly is more highly-priced because someone else made it! It'll furthermore help you clearly distinguish how an lousy lot you actually need to spend on meals as opposed to what's immoderate. And, certain, you ought to genuinely depend that tumbler of espresso you get in your manner to artwork within the morning, even though it's now not anything more than a -greenback charge!

Entertainment—You don't should don't forget books or music in this class, due to the fact you could need to check those subjects as being device for self-improvement. However, a stay overall performance or a film, a few component spent inside the name of entertainment would fall under 'entertainment.' The lottery counts, so placed your tickets in here too, if you buy them. You might also additionally additionally or won't select out to place your health club club or any type of enjoyment workout on this class. This is absolutely as a good buy as you. Some may also moreover moreover preserve in thoughts these sports activities as part of the preventative health costs we were speaking approximately earlier. At the same time, you could in some unspecified time inside the destiny decide to honestly training consultation from home and bypass the choose-up football video games only for this season or create a unfastened league among buddies.

Child costs—The expenses your youngsters require may also additionally moreover a few months look like they rival that of your loan! From diapers to toys to highschool property to tuition charges, those are going to be most vital charges to regulate sooner or later of the years, in case you want to stay on pinnacle of your price range and debt. We have an entire monetary spoil dedicated to discern-budgeting arising!

Debt—Depending on the manner you feel about this class, you may locate that you'd need to location your loan proper here. We'll pass into greater details about debt manipulate in a later bankruptcy. Just apprehend that the way you classify the loan is in reality as heaps as you. You can also find which you're pressing to eliminate it, and so you positioned it here. Maybe you have got have been given a accomplice, however, who's now not as worried as long as fairness is accruing. In that case, counting on something techniques you operate, you could record it in a way that suits you each at the same time as not having it depend two instances for your fees. For each unique sort of debt you owe, endure in thoughts the interest costs on each. In fact, you may need to mark them down beside their respective money owed. This is essential, due to the fact, in the end, the interest plus the capital is what you owe, not genuinely the capital on my own. Bearing that during mind will preserve the texture of urgency you've got got closer to paying off your debt that a whole lot more potent.

Savings—Start with what you presently are saving now, and sincerely don't forget beginning an emergency fund, in case you haven't already. We'll talk extra approximately purpose putting and financial financial savings a piece later, but for now, even if you don't have the extra cash, take what you're already saving, and element out a number of it for a wet day. Consider what else you is probably saving in the course of, and don't neglect any part of your earnings this is deducted in the direction of your paintings or government pension. Not the entirety this is taken off of your gross earnings is exactly going towards taxes. Double check your pay stub!

Seasonal expenses—This can be any other discretionary kind of price in that you set aside a small amount each month to move in the route of things like garments, upkeep, journeying charges, and a few issue else that requires a quarterly fee.

Business costs—If you're in business commercial enterprise company for yourself otherwise you're self-employed, then you definately honestly're in all likelihood already properly versed in budgeting on your commercial company costs. Most every industrial enterprise may be very worried with keeping charges at a minimal in order to maximize income. Not every enterprise company individual is finance savvy, but, so that you can also want to live tuned for the financial disaster on budgeting along side your industrial business enterprise in mind. You'll be considering such things as materials and other inventory, searching after your personnel or your very personal hard work, management and taxes, and so forth.

Charity—You may furthermore have already categorized those charges into non-public or residing prices, mainly if tithing can be very important to you for your faith. Any donations may also even fall under this beauty, and make sure to bear in mind any tax credit score you can acquire for having contributed to a charitable company.

Don't neglect to thing in your costs that come quarterly, if no longer seasonally, or even yearly for that rely. Putting a touch away each month might be beneficial and further inexperienced for you.

Step 3: Differentiate Between Your Income and Expenses

After you've finished steps one and , differentiating among your earnings and fees must be obvious at this aspect. So some distance, it's no longer essential to try to correct something or create an 'excellent' price range plan. If you've listed subjects simply as they'll be, the corrections you are making developing might be all the greater powerful at the same time as implementing them.

When doing this step, you may find out little to no financial savings to be had, or you may even understand you're at a deficit. This can take place in case you rely too intently on credit score score gambling cards to tide you over all through the month while your subsequent paycheck hasn't are available in but. Coming to this reputation can be in reality dreadful and disheartening; it would make you give up on your goals altogether. To this, we are saying: Don't lose preference. You're no longer the excellent one in this seize 22 state of affairs, even in case you don't pay interest approximately every person else's cash struggles. That being said, you've probably additionally heard tales of humans coming once more after exorbitant portions of debt to live the life they want to now. Using a fee range may be step one in turning into this sort of humans, however you do have to start. The element approximately cash is that the longer you put off searching after its troubles, the larger those issues emerge as over the lengthy haul. Money is sort of a lawn: If you diligently will be inclined to it, it'll be stunning and bountiful, however depart it too prolonged, and weeds will sprout on their very own and take over with none help from you.

Some Solutions to No Savings and Too Much Debt

The obvious solution would be to each cut returned on a number of your expenses or discover a manner to make extra money. We all recognise that more money is a completely useful answer! However, if you're not already managing the cash you have were given now, possibilities are that with a bigger paycheck, you'll handiest discover yourself knee-deep in large troubles.

Now which you've determined to deal with the charges on your budget, you would possibly want to apply some of the questions we went thru in bankruptcy one concerning reducing or disposing of some of these devices.

Can you stay a few one of a kind region? Unless you're a younger pupil who can more with out hassle leap from one area to the subsequent, this one, notwithstanding the reality that first at the list, should maximum probable be a remaining lodge in an try and live below your method. Nevertheless, if you've come to some extent where you're no matter the truth that struggling to make your payments no matter doing the whole lot right, it is probably time to preserve in mind the truth that you can't manage to pay for to stay inside the region you do now. Downsizing is probably more feasible to an older couple or a single character, however this by myself must take away a incredible bite of your economic responsibility.

Can you buy superb essential gadgets in bulk? While searching for in bulk necessitates spending greater at one time, it would ease the stress to your price range over time. Things like lavatory paper or girl merchandise are things you will possibly need to keep in thoughts purchasing for in bulk, in view that you apprehend you'll always need them. Think about bulking up on the pricier meals of your grocery list as nicely. Items like meat and seafood may be stored to your freezer and used over the years.

Can you turn economic organization accounts? Finding the right financial organization account for you is probably complex and tedious at the beginning, however well nicely worth it ultimately. Having a financial organization account with minimum costs usually way the quantity of transactions you may do are restrained. Likewise, having unlimited transaction capacity in a financial institution account typically manner you need to keep up with their stability limit requirements. For example, if you have to hold as a minimum $1,000 in a monetary institution account, this could assist you amplify the dependancy of fending off overdraft on the same time as keeping a chunk cushion for your emergency fund. Take the time to find out a economic institution account that'll wholesome your price variety, but that permits you to furthermore assist preserve proper behavior.

Can you stroll? We may be in the addiction of taking our car anywhere, so heading over to the nook shop through foot is probably a pleasing change in your pockets and your health (there are those preventative measures, over again!). Also, remember taking public transit in which you can. Consider the space from paintings. Taking the bus might be much less steeply-priced over the month than the quantity of gas you'd pay, and also you'd be able to get a few analyzing finished too!

Can you get a higher charge? Shop spherical for prices collectively together with your insurances, or the first rate forms of subscriptions and memberships you hold.

Can you placed my 'desires' on preserve only for a bit even as? Check out that list of nonessentials now and notice if some aspect falls under the non-public, leisure, or eating out lessons. Verify which sports sports may be placed on keep for a duration of 3 to six months. If you have a particular motive in thoughts for the cash you'll save, preserving it in thoughts may also assist you keep motivation all through that length.

Can you get it 2nd-hand? Hunt up garage sales, thrift stores, or maybe your dad's closet! What are a few objects you want that don't require you to pay full charge at retail?

Can you consolidate a number of your debt? While the possibility of every other mortgage or a re-mortgage is intimidating sufficient, if you schooling consultation a plan at the facet of your loaner, it would save you time and interest at the decrease again-prevent. If you consolidate effectively and keep on with the plan, you can create more savings or pay above your minimal bills. The former gets you rich quicker, on the identical time due to the fact the latter gets you out of debt quicker. Can you do each at the identical time? Talk to a expert for help with this form of plan, and stay tuned for that debt manipulate bankruptcy. You need to ensure you're doing topics correctly.

Feel unfastened to invite your self those questions even if you have no deficit or any hassle saving. The more you may optimize your plan, the quicker and the easier it'll be on the manner to benefit the type of wealth you're after.

Step 4: Assign Spending Amounts for Each Category

This step is fantastically brief, due to the fact you've already amassed how a good buy you're spending in every category. Having completed step three, you've already got an concept of strategies an awful lot you'd like to spend inside the numerous regions of your life. Once you've consistent an amount for each elegance, it's now your assignment to not pass over that quantity. If you've spent the quantity of cash you need for toiletries, as an example, you want to discover ways to make do with rationing that toothpaste for the relaxation of the month!

As you've made a clear listing of your important charges, maintain that listing of nonessentials, even in case you're no longer going to be spending in that place for some time. If you're the use of a spreadsheet, you can use a strikethrough in the ones nonessential line gadgets. The reason being is that in case you plan to begin spending within the ones areas yet again, you'll need to trouble in those prices earlier of time. If you do determine to hold spending on nice nonessential gadgets, reason out their fee and make certain their fee is surely worth it to you. For example, a gymnasium membership, while nonessential to a few, is probably essential for your power and ordinary intellectual health. As long as you're the use of it for what it's nicely really worth, don't sense responsible approximately this cash spent—use it nicely!

The following is a popular breakdown of processes cash need to be spent. We'll communicate approximately making comparisons to others within the monetary catastrophe on coins mentality, but for now, this manual is meant certainly as a reference, and no longer as a grading machine to decide how well you're doing. Take what you need, and leave the rest. The listing is broken down into possibilities of your earnings:

• Living costs—about 35%

• Utilities—5%

• Transportation—15%–20%

- Food—10%–20%

- Debt—five%–15%

- Personal and amusement—5%–10%

- Savings—five%–10%

- Clothing and other seasonal purchases—three%–5%

- Medical/Health—three%

Whether or no longer you spend in every elegance each month doesn't remember. This listing indicates a breakdown of what you want to located away each month for every category's purpose. For instance, you won't take your circle of relatives out to dinner 3 months in a row, but in month four, you have got four months well worth of monthly economic monetary savings in that elegance to apply. You can move all out for that one night time, or just use a number of the fee variety and hold the relaxation for some other super night time.

Another word to make is that in case your debt payments exceed 15% of your earnings, based in this breakdown, then that is a sturdy indicator that your money owed are out of hand, and you is probably within the position to don't forget a downgrade of life-style or a consolidation. You need to truely are searching for advice from a loan expert or your economic representative.

Step five: Determine a Purpose for Your Savings

This is in which you can make all your efforts so far don't forget variety. You don't want in reality all of us telling you which you need to save, however don't forget what you are saving for and at the equal time as, in addition to how heaps it'll fee. If you haven't finished this little little little bit of intention setting but, then now might be an brilliant time to at least get a huge concept of it going.

What do you need? When do you want it? How a superb deal does it fee? Additionally, you'll in all likelihood undergo in thoughts asking yourself what you're willing to do to make the ones goals show up. Are you surely geared up to alternate your behavior?

Having an Emergency Fund

Having an emergency fund is so vital. If you find out your self in credit score score card debt, then it's probably due to the truth you as soon as had an emergency that required more price variety than you've got got been capable of offer at one time. Starting an emergency fund and in reality heading off its use will prevent from completing in an sudden hole in the future. You would probably assume which you'd want to throw every remaining penny in the route of your debt. However, doing as a way to leave you without a cushion to fall again on while an emergency does stand up. You'll want to bypass again into the debt you have been striving so difficult to do away with inside the first area.

Short-Term Goals

You can also want to store toward any quick-time period dreams that may encompass becoming debt free, in which you'd be spending your greater monetary savings to your debt. This is a fantastic idea, so don't give up! Paying over your debt's minimum bills will ensure that any overages move completely in the direction of the capital of your debt and no hobby or charges. This will let you get out of debt extra rapid and store on that interest.

Medium and Long-Term Goals

These desires are ones which you're seeking to reach within the subsequent 3 to five years and past. They are in all likelihood the maximum interesting, no longer to say hefty, due to the fact they typically must do with retirement, tour, or things of that nature. These are goals in that you get to do together together together with your time as you please. That being said, take into account your retirement as an additional-lengthy holiday (which it's miles). If you've executed any planning for a journey overseas, then you definitely truely understand how time-eating that form of planning is, and just how pricey that journey might be. Your retirement isn't any unique, and in fact, ought to include the relative quantity of time and hobby in the direction of its making plans. Don't make the mistake of questioning you have got time whilst time is definitely the precept element that'll decide without a doubt how an awful lot you get to spend inside the route of retirement. More on saving and making an funding later!

Step 6: Make It a Habit

Having the sector to live steady with the right conduct will will assist you to have success in any shape of challenge or capability. Here are a few behavior to set up as you begin your budgeting workout plan. Remember, this isn't about punishing yourself, or searching for to "be appropriate." This is prepared conducting your monetary dreams and becoming free financially.

Continue to Track Your Expenses

Make certain to log every single purchase or transaction you're making. This looks like overkill, however if you're new to budgeting, otherwise you discover it's now not wherein your strengths lie, then it can be a piece complex to get the cling of it in the starting. If you forget approximately your plan, you run the hazard of giving up on it earlier than you've given it enough time to clearly make a difference. That being said, don't beat your self up both in case you've disregarded a few element, or in case you've commenced out on the incorrect foot. The trick here is to ensure you're really trying and now not brushing off a few issue. How intentional you are at the begin will assist decide how probable you are to conform with through till the give up.

Be sure to log the whole lot of their respective education; you would possibly find out yourself being extra vigilant within the beginning because of the fact you're just being used to the device. Take have a examine of a few thing that doesn't fit you or find out tough to examine or use. These notes can assist making a decision if your tool is operating well for you, or in case you want to alternate it up a bit bit. File away all of your receipts in a chosen basket or document folder on the manner to document later. Likewise, make certain to download any receipts or invoices you've received electronically proper right into a document to your computer. It permits to time desk a excellent time of the day for logging in transactions into the budgeting tool. Doing this at the equal time every day will help solidify the dependancy and could affirm to yourself that you're essential about this new device. This doesn't have to take lengthy, certainly take some thing receipts or invoices you've gathered finally of the day and log them in. You can appearance over the actual budget and decide if your plan is going without problems at the prevent of each week. Again, time table a specific time for this as nicely. Since this may take a piece greater time, it might be first rate to have time set apart in which you're undisturbed. A useful tip might be to set an alarm for your smartphone indicating that it's time to each go online your transactions at the give up of the day, or to transport over your fee range plan at the quit of the week. Budgeting will fast become second nature to you.

You also can or may not discover that maintaining in reality the whole lot finance related for your budgeting plan to be useful to you. Including records regarding your taxes and pension plans multi feature place might be handy inside the experience that you'll be capable of have an customary view of strategies you're doing in a single appearance. If it, but, is certainly too overwhelming and receives you pressured, then it's probable now not nicely well really worth it.

Stick to Your Budget

Once you've were given the hold of actually the use of your budgeting plan, maintain to paste to the manner and show your plan each week. You may also revel in confident enough to loosen up together together with your surveillance and feature a examine the whole lot as quickly as each weeks. Keep in mind in case you've used up all the fee variety in a sure elegance you need to save you spending in that magnificence for the month, but you could discover you need to lend from some other class to make your bills. If that's the case, are you capable of top off what you borrowed from the opportunity class quickly after. Or are you capable of genuinely stop spending inside the class you borrowed from? The idea is to not need to scramble to discover the extra money to pay on your purchases. This form of tendency is precisely what we're trying to cast off the usage of the rate range.

Track Your Progress

Not best need to you be monitoring your prices, however you ought to moreover tune your development and feature fun any and all milestones. Depending on how a good deal disposable profits you've got, it might be really genuinely worth growing a rewards category to your fee range to use whenever you've performed a milestone in your plan. Celebrating gives you a boost of self guarantee and gratitude, and an warranty which you're at the proper song. This will offer you with the motivation you need to keep cementing the addiction of budgeting into your lifestyles.

Keep a replica of the original evaluation of your budget and evaluate it to the budgeting plan you've set up place for yourself. As you continue to live diligent and disciplined, you'll see month after month certainly how an extended way you've come. You might not even understand your monetary situation six months from now. Try to don't forget the feelings and doubts you had at the start of this venture. We frequently don't get started with a few trouble, despite the fact that we really want to do it, due to the truth we accept as true with that we are able to't, or that not something will without a doubt acquired't art work or make a distinction. Remembering your preliminary thoughts and the way they modified will assist you recognize the power of development and what a smooth charge variety can do.

Adjust your budget whenever something adjustments, collectively with you get a growth otherwise you free up more earnings after having cleared a debt. The extra you figure the plan, the quicker you'll construct momentum. Most importantly, have a laugh the ones wins!

Extra Budgeting Tips

Here are only a few greater pointers you could use whilst setting your plan together.

Your Social Calendar

Keep your social sports in mind almost about budgeting—that is one we're able to effects neglect about. Before the beginning of each new budgeting month, ask yourself if there are any birthdays or potlucks this month. Prepare ahead of time for the numerous vacation seasons you could have an awesome time, further to for the summer time months in which people will be inclined to have extra outings and sports.

Your Emergency Fund

By now, you've have been given a clean image of simply how vital the emergency fund is. If you find your finances is simply too tight to undergo in mind a massive emergency fund, then determine to set aside as a minimum $1,000 in case of emergencies. Make wonderful you only ever remember using this cash for financially hefty emergencies, like an twist of fate or clinical emergency. This fund is for huge issues most effective. Once you're debt loose, then you could begin to have a take a look at developing a bigger emergency fund, usually three to six months honestly well worth of profits. This will assist in conditions wherein the insurance on an twist of destiny won't come thru or unemployment occurs. If you do want to use it, pinnacle off it as speedy as feasible. Whether you located it in a excessive, balanced, or low yield funding fund is in your discretion. While many want to ensure that the quantity of coins they want is normally to be had, others enjoy comfortable making an investment this cash due to the reality otherwise it's simply sitting there.

Cash Flow

If you've got a complicated cash go with the flow, as an example, you nice gets a fee as quickly as a month or on the stop of each task, then be sure to divide your earnings consistent with your charge schedules. You understand what your essentials (fixed and variable) are and at the equal time as you want to pay them, so keep the cash required to honor those bills in a separate account till you're ready to pay them. When you dinner party (recollect that analogy?), set apart a number of the ones quantities for while there may be a famine. Always maintain your priorities smooth.

Supplement Your Income

Do you locate you're in reality now not making sufficient? Are there any opportunities to work from home at your personal pace that you may pursue? Think of hard work in editing, writing, or tutoring on line. Look into trying seasonal or element-time paintings. Where you may, motive to elevate your rate as an man or woman. The more revel in you have were given under your belt, the a good deal less complicated it'll be to be able to ask for what you deserve even as inquiring for a increase or looking for a advertising and advertising and marketing.

Pay Yourself First

Whenever you may, pay yourself first. Just much like the authorities takes its taxes in advance than your paycheck even reaches you, you and your circle of relatives ought to be a top precedence. While you do have your right away times to recollect, and we have been talking approximately getting easy in your priorities, in case you're in a role, make saving one of those pinnacle priorities. After all of the invoice paying is completed, it's too tempting to spend some thing is left. We've labored difficult all month, and there's only a lot of our paycheck left whilst we've taken care of our obligations. Wanting to indulge is natural. However, in case you don't stay with your plan, you'll find out yourself inside the same function you've continuously been in with little to no cash left over for you on the forestall of the month. The purpose is freedom—staying diligent now will assist you to be freed from some of those obligations inside the destiny. When you do all you may you're bringing that freedom to yourself that lots faster.

Budgeting Strategies

As we've mentioned, there are numerous techniques to fee range that depend upon your manner of life and options. Basically, understanding your very own fashion of running will assist to make the budgeting approach as green and as painless as viable. When you understand your self and the way amazing you function, things run more easily and also you react efficaciously. It's a good deal less complicated, then, to make the tough picks to be able to will assist you to march more abruptly towards your financial freedom.

Here's a clean summary to remind you of the elements which can be required in each form of finances no matter your fashion. You want your economic savings bills, and prioritize paying your self first on every occasion you can. Consider your economic savings account a bill you owe your self towards a future life-style. Housing, utilities, and transportation are all lessons to encompass for your rate variety; don't forget about any fees or taxes that go together with the ones education. Food, non-public care, and a few different dwelling prices bypass on your lists as well, or even the random experience to Starbucks counts. Your debts are an vital a part of your budgeting plan as you nicely apprehend, but if you're clearly looking to get out of debt as rapid as feasible, you truely need to determine to the discontinued use of credit score. If you wind up falling once more on credit rating due to the fact you didn't create an emergency or miscellaneous fund, in any other case you really can't face up to an unplanned buy, then severa your artwork may also want to have lengthy past out the window. Any insurances or one of a kind healthcare prices are well really worth mastering after you've determined their position for your fee range. This magnificence can get luxurious, however it's regularly vital. So ensure that you've were given the right products for you, and that the fees you pay are honestly nicely well worth the price you acquire. Finally, there's enjoyment and leisure prices to embody in your rate variety. Keeping a miscellaneous elegance is the non-obligatory class, however the trick to identifying its use for your price range will be to preserve all of your receipts for the first few months, and then you definately definately definately'll be higher capable of decide if you're justified in growing the greater elegance.

Now, allow's test the best-of-a-kind budgeting strategies you may strive. Think approximately your very very own behavior and behaviors, in addition to the way you trust you studied via solving a problem. This will help you make a decision what form of budgeting fashion is proper for you. Your charge range is also your opportunity to observe yourself so to talk. You'll get to realise in which your inclined spots are, so attempting severa forms of budgeting is probably properly really worth the trial and errors at the begin. Give each fashion a danger.

Zero-Based Budgeting

What this approach manner is that each dollar to your budget has a reason and need to be used up for that purpose through using the give up of the month. Spending every unmarried greenback you earn this month may additionally moreover sound amusing if a bit reckless, however the roles you assign every of your greenbacks ought to need to do with saving or debt bills. The concept is that even in case you find out yourself with $2.Sixty 3 more for your economic employer account, you have to assign that unique amount somewhere based totally totally for your plan. The amount of cash coming in is the proper identical sum of money that's going out.

This technique is remarkable for someone who's distinctly stimulated to pay off their money owed and start saving as an extended-term dependancy. Doing topics in this way also takes a chunk greater attempt than the opposite techniques we'll have a examine, further to lots of time spent monitoring money owed and transactions. You'd want to set apart the time to do the whole thing way earlier, and are looking for recommendation out of your plan regularly earlier than making any monetary picks. This way, you keep away from making impulse purchases, making sure which you continuously have sufficient for what you've deliberate for.

You may additionally choose out out to go along with this style of budgeting for an entire lot of reasons. You may also already be a completely organized and no-nonsense form of individual in terms of dealing with your private affairs. On the other hand, you may also be someone who's no longer prepared in any respect and looking to create a bit of duty for your self. If you understand which you need to have a chunk greater care together along with your budget and be greater accountable, then you definately definately might also additionally additionally pick out this technique. This will be a big shift for you than for the person that's already very strict with themselves, so do not forget of the transition to turning into extra detail-orientated. You don't need to provide your self a difficult time, specially on the start of this new trade.

Bucket Budget or the 50/30/20 Budget

Bucket budgeting includes placing your diverse instructions into 3 first rate buckets. A bucket in your goals, some other in your dreams, and yet every other on your financial savings and money owed. Ideally, 50% of your profits is going into the wishes bucket, 30% into the bucket of needs, and the ultimate 20% into the bucket first rate for economic financial savings and debts. If you locate that stability is essential in your sanity, this price range is brilliant ideal for you! Sometimes being strict like with 0-based definitely budgeting can simplest art work for goodbye earlier than you discover your self itching to "stay a chunk." Much like a strict weight loss program, you can find out that you may't hold that type of way of lifestyles, and so that you snap, taking place an ingesting binge. The identical element also can want to take region financially. If you recognize you're the kind of individual who wishes a bit of consolation and simplicity to manual you in the times while you're more vigilant together along with your cash, then developing some area for indulgent spending is accurate. Bucket budgeting on this way allow you to to not sense responsible approximately the luxurious objects or impulses you've had this month. You get to have a bit a few factor for yourself now on the same time as notwithstanding the fact that sticking to a plan for your destiny.

Budgeting doesn't have to be strict, but should instead mold itself for your way of life and manner of being. You can also find out, in fact, that zero-based totally absolutely budgeting is what you want for as a minimum the primary or 3 months of your recreation plan. Once you have your footing with budgeting, you can then transition into bucket budgeting for a piece greater wiggle room and coins to loosen up. Feel unfastened to exchange up the chances if need be; you could find out you want to break up the bucket in a selected way. For instance, 60% of your profits goes into the needs bucket, on the identical time because the very last forty% is break up equally amongst goals and economic financial savings and money owed. Likewise, you may switch up the manner the coins is allocated with the useful resource of putting 30% of your profits toward financial savings and debts, while the final 20% goes toward desires. This is as a first-rate deal as you, and also you'll likely analyze what chances and lessons are pleasant in your scenario after a few months of recording your costs.

Envelope System

You might also additionally moreover have already got an idea as to what this approach includes, and you can have thoroughly seen your mother and father or grandparents stay on this manner. What you do is call an envelope for each class you've indexed on your charge variety sheet. Then, you location the amount of cash in coins which you've assigned for every category in its genuine envelope. Once that envelope runs out of cash, spending in that elegance additionally ends for the month.

If you have got trouble controlling your use of credit score rating playing cards, you'll possibly discover this approach useful. In the world of credit score score score and debit, cash isn't a sum of bills and coins anymore. It's frequently too smooth to swipe a card without in reality figuring out how masses we're converting. The envelope device is a completely tactile way of handling your charge range. When you literally ought to cope with your cash to your palms, you is probably capable of get a higher experience of the way loads coins you sincerely use on a month-to-month basis. It's moreover very visible which may be useful to you in the first actual months of searching for to have a observe a fee variety. When cash becomes "out of sight, out of thoughts" adore it often is in recent times within the digital global, we often neglect about that we've got got monetary desires initially.

This tool also can be a completely useful schooling device if you have a more younger own family. If you maintain the envelopes in a place in which your youngsters will see them, it's an opportunity to allow them to realise what you're doing and why. They'll see what you're doing month after month, and may even maintain you accountable in your goals in the occasion that they phrase you've ignored your envelopes. We all understand that children whether or not they're toddlers or teens regularly don't pay attention or do what you inform them. They do have a observe with the aid of manner of mimicking, but, especially the youngest of babies. Even the oldest of teens will (hundreds to their private chagrin) do what you do. If your kids see you doing some component green and current for yourself, they will follow healthy and discover ways to moreover be powerful and revolutionary for themselves. The first rate manner to make certain your kids come to be all they may be is thru manner of first becoming all you'll be your self.

Here's a in addition tip approximately the envelope machine: Using coins for each form of transaction or charge might be inconvenient or maybe now not viable. In that case, use apps like Goodbudget or Mvelopes. With those apps, you can securely link up your financial institution debts to be able to create virtual envelopes much like you'll with real ones.

Reverse Budget

With the other budgeting approach, you without a doubt should begin with the motive thoughts. The idea with this approach is which you're prioritizing your destiny or most vital goals before something else. That is your month-to-month spending price range is based totally definitely surely in your economic financial savings plans and economic goals. How that works is you decide what goals you really need to accumulate. You then want to determine out how a whole lot they'd every fee, further to how thousands that might require you to maintain each month. If you have got a retirement aim or you really want to ensure your kids have sufficient for university whilst the time comes, you'd pay the month-to-month requirements into your first rate financial financial savings bills every month first. Whatever coins is final after this is the amount of coins you'll ought to live on. You're no longer neglecting the needs and responsibilities you've got now, of course. You definitely don't permit the rate of your maximum instant prices consume into the charge of your lengthy-term dreams.

This technique in reality takes dwelling interior your technique to a modern-day level. This technique has a tendency to be for the sort of man or woman who's already extraordinarily stimulated with the aid of the use of their goals. The very last results they need is plain, and they don't constantly experience the want to stay for now if it manner probably jeopardizing or maybe delaying their desires later. Once you emerge as greater disciplined and characteristic a higher concept of wherein you'd like your existence to transport, you can discover it feasible to strive your hand at opposite budgeting. This form of budgeting device is definitely for the kind of character who's centered with an prolonged-term outlook. This method can also be great for a person who's out of debt and is already quite satisfied with their current-day manner of life. If you've got got debt or are though struggling with assembly your essential desires, then this approach is probably too demanding for you proper now.

Five-Category Budget

If your head is spinning with any of the techniques we've pointed out to this point, then you can just like the five-category finances as it's extra smooth. You'll be splitting your spending into five fundamental classes: housing, transportation, some exclusive dwelling expenses (which includes any discretionary spending), monetary financial savings, and ultimately debt. If you experience you're not high-quality wherein to begin as a primary-time budgeter, in any other case you discover huge sheets with strains and contours of objects and classes intimidating, then you definitely actually'll probable respect this form of technique. It's clean to document and document away every of your fees while not having to think through every single detail.

This smooth technique is awesome for the form of person who has a low earnings, or who appreciates dwelling surely. They have easy goals and modest dreams and are in reality content cloth with what they presently have moving into their existence. This may be perfect for a extra youthful, unmarried individual who's constantly jogging or studying or each. You in all likelihood haven't any dependents in the interim, and so not many charges which can be variable or sudden. This method you wouldn't need to spend that a wonderful deal time budgeting, and might maximum probably record and prepare everything on payday. After that, you may go lower again to focusing to your paintings and studies. Keep in thoughts, in case you're the busy kind, you most possibly aren't an impulse consumer. That being said, in case you worry approximately staying accountable on your price variety however do want to keep subjects easy, then it is probably well really worth including multiple sub-classes to the debt and unique dwelling costs categories. You'll although hold the simplicity of the five number one instructions, but can still strategize awesome schooling in a way that enables you manipulate your lousy behavior and get out of debt. For instance, the manner you control the kinds of housing, transportation, and savings can stay clean, on the identical time as you follow the 0-based totally approach to the varieties of wonderful dwelling fees and debts.

10% Buffer Budget

This budgeting technique is a totally bendy one and also can be complemented to one-of-a-kind types of strategies. This method truely dictates that you fee range 90% of your earnings, at the equal time as leaving your self a buffer with the very last 10%. This 10% may be used as an emergency fund, or you may dip into it in case you find you're lacking fee range in a few commands for the month. This is proper for the individual with a number of variable charges or earnings.

This method is right for the form of individual who has some problem with retaining their impulsive spending in take a look at. If you find out you're sincerely struggling with debt or with the addiction of saving, you then definately moreover might also find out this method perfect for you. If you could, you then certainly could possibly find out it beneficial to fake which you actually only make 90% of what you take domestic. If you keep that ninety% discern in mind, then you certainly in reality're more likely to live internal that quantity of coins. Rather than faux, you would possibly locate it more powerful to preserve 10% of your income from your draw near. This technique automatically saving it into an account that might then make the cash tough to liquidate. That is, if you had to fill in paperwork or wait 3 to five industrial employer days on every occasion you preferred to access this cash, you can actually renounce your self to finding some other manner of getting the money, or without a doubt waiting till you've got got the quantity you need. In this situation, you'd technically be budgeting the 10% away and basically paying your self first, however taking this type of angle of downgrading how a bargain you genuinely make could probable help you with overspending.

You can without troubles pair this method up with any of the opportunity techniques. For instance, you may pick to fee range that 90% of your income using the bucket approach. That is, of the ninety%, 50% is going closer to your goals, 30% to your desires, and then 20% for your money owed and monetary savings. You can likewise, control 90% of your income in the 0-based totally absolutely way. The 10% buffer you supply yourself will permit you the gap to discover which method is notable for you.

How Do You Choose Which Budget Is Right for You?

Before doing a little component, it's exceptional to check that initial evaluation of your price range from chapters one and . It'd be tough to determine at the fantastic direction of motion if you're no longer precisely certain in which you stand. After that evaluation, decide wherein your weaknesses are; notwithstanding the fact that, you can already have a wonderful concept about human beings with out the want of an evaluation. Decide what your lousy conduct are, and if you'd want to trade any of them, select out out which ones you may discover the money for to alternate proper away. You may find out there are a few behavior that is probably better modified through the years.

A self-evaluation doesn't have to be all doom and gloom. Take a take a look at your top conduct similarly in your goals, and note if there's a way to apply them to offset the behaviors which are hurting you. You want to moreover don't forget your values. Does your child's training without a doubt rely to you? Do you want residing a pleasing manner of lifestyles now? Do you opt for eating properly over having cloth possessions? If you understand those gadgets about yourself, you'll be better able to decide which type of technique or mixture of techniques is proper for you.

Consider additionally how geared up and inclined you are to exchange! Remember, if you sense you're doing this really due to the truth you understand you have to, then the threat of you staying consistent on the side of your finances could likely lower. Unless you have a real and considerable purpose for organizing your monetary duties, it'll be difficult to paste to the fee range.

Do you discover you need to use paper, or do you do the whole lot to your cellular telephone except and so pick an app? Maybe you're a chunk of an Excel sheet nerd, and could use a spreadsheet in your budgeting wishes. Personalize your finances to residence the manner you stay and count on, and personalize your approach to fit your desires and way of lifestyles. You'll increase the chance of your consistency with the plan, and you'll moreover experience like your desires are being met.

For instance, possibly you're surely outstanding at planning and organizing, but you like ingesting out or frequenting new restaurants. In that case, in choice to consuming out every time you'd like, plan a go to to a latest restaurant you'd like to strive every time you've reached a milestone in your price range.

More Budgeting Tips

Here are a few extra ideas so that you can embody inside the execution of your budgeting game plan. If any of them resonate with you, use them at your very own consolation. Making a addiction of any person of those pointers should allow you to ease into the dependancy of budgeting, mainly if you've usually had hassle sticking to a plan, or when you have hassle believing that your plan may additionally want to clearly make a difference for you. With all of the recommendation in this e-book, take what you can, and go away what doesn't art work. This isn't about averting mistakes and bad conduct, or following your plan to a tee. This is ready growing in your self a experience of self-self assure in terms of your charge variety and an guarantee that the dreams you plan out may be executed with the mission to stay everyday.

A Miscellaneous Category

If this is your first actual attempt at sticking to a price range, and you're having hassle planning matters out, you would possibly need to create a class for miscellaneous spending no matter what sort of budgeting style you choose to start off with. Even if you've long long past via all of your spending inside the past few months or yr for you to accumulate an idea of what your spending is like, it'd nevertheless be tricky to get a true control on what transactions to anticipate.

You might also moreover do all the making plans you could, and despite the fact that find out masses of unexpected items wind up for your price variety that you didn't foresee. This can be very irritating to you, specifically if budgeting receives you fearful or makes you doubt yourself. For the annoying first-timers, create a miscellaneous magnificence in that you place that 10% buffer that we stated inside the last segment as one of the budgeting techniques you can enforce.

After 3 or four months, if you be conscious that some of those purchases within the miscellaneous elegance preserve showing up, then you can remember placing them in one in each of your set up categories. You also can even discover that you have to name an entire new category for the ones transactions. The concept in the lower back of this miscellaneous elegance is that it'll assist you get the hold of budgeting on the equal time as presenting you with a piece more clarity at the way you spend your lifestyle.

Automatic Payments

You probably have already got wonderful payments or payments which may be mechanically deducted out of your economic organization account. Consider doing this with each unmarried considered considered one of your payments, mainly those bills that ought to do on the aspect of your funding and saving priorities. If you are making those commitments in advance of time, you're more likely to take your personal priorities seriously. Be high-quality to moreover make automatic bills on your emergency and leisure and entertainment budget. If you're being too strict with your self, you may in the destiny discover your self at your wits surrender of field, and indulge with the useful useful resource of taking cash from your funding and saving debts. These sorts of moves aren't most effective damaging to growing your budgeting behavior, but additionally for your lengthy-time period dreams. If your prolonged-term monetary savings are being eaten away grade by grade over a time period, the very last effects you had been expecting to your lengthy-term dreams may additionally want to in reality end up very disappointing.

Like with the alarms you could pick out to set for your self as reminders of while it's time to log in purchases or to head over your price range, supply your self reminders of while you'll have upcoming computerized withdrawals for your account. That way, you'll be reminded of the following movements you'll be making on your price range, and you can affirm that you have the right quantity of fee variety and that the whole lot is going according to plot. This is especially vital for bills closer to credit score playing gambling playing cards and other money owed as you'll need to have the ones paid properly earlier than their due date. This is crucial for maintaining a healthy credit score score, which we'll communicate approximately inside the next chapter.

For items on your budget that could't without a doubt be placed on an automatic device, attempt growing a list of these costs which you're remarkable of, in addition to their charge. Grocery devices, for example, are clean sufficient to listing, and you could decide on them in advance of time. Once the time includes make your purchases, head to the shops with simply the proper sum of money (use cash whilst you could). You can encompass a buffer or enough cash for miscellaneous purchases, however the concept is which you do your shopping for with very precise instructions. This will reduce the chances of impulse buys or splurging. Your prone factor for cookies and ice cream need to be factored into your price range, and it might surely be unwise to attempt to exclude them, however greater wholesome that choice can be. Unless you're simultaneously running to your fitness dreams, it's in all likelihood fine to budget your areas of weak spot instead of trying to deny them. Denying them will high-quality almost assure an oncoming splurge. While health goals are beyond the scope of this ebook, it's vital to word that the massive addiction shifts you're searching for to create are superb achieved one by one and regularly. You can be excited to your newly deliberate goals and the opportunities of living a existence that's more authentic to what you take into account, but don't overlook that the call of the game to lengthy-lasting alternate—as traumatic as it is—is to domesticate your new self a touch bit at a time. The basis is continuously the longest phase of constructing the residence, but as soon as it's performed proper, the relaxation of the house comes together fast and lasts for a long time. So, keep in thoughts: Automatic bills are approximately helping you installation that foundation for absolutely changing your conduct.

Prioritize Purpose

People who stay more useful lives will be inclined to be happier and more fulfilled with who they will be. Being at paintings day in and time out can also motive us to lose sight of that cause we're looking to reap. It can also feel like we don't truely have that huge of a cause, besides seeing our family thru every other round of month-to-month payments, ensuring the whole thing receives paid on time and really every body receives what they want.

Giving and saving, therefore, regularly take a backseat to our budgeting plans. We might also furthermore experience much like the cash we'd want to allot to the ones features ought to very well assist repay the debt we're swimming in instead. The notable we do with our cash, but, can help inspire the other tremendous behaviors we'd like to set up with our spending. This isn't to mention that you need to tithe on the equal time as you in reality haven't any disposable earnings, or deliver away more money while you can truly be accelerating debt. This is truly a name a excellent manner to make certain that what you're spending is intentional, useful, and effective. The more beneficial you sense with your coins, the greater empowered you'll be to preserve executing the plan that'll promote your wealth.

Stay Flexible

Don't fall in love together together along with your budgeting plan! Staying flexible across the manner you execute some issue it is which you plan is the way you increase the chance of prolonged-time period success. Ironically sufficient, it is able to are also to be had in handy to keep your expectancies of your goals free as properly.

While you're likely looking to create economic independence, this may look one-of-a-type for simply anybody and might even exchange over the years to your very very own eyes as nicely. How you go approximately attaining your goals will constantly alternate primarily based mostly on what you discover approximately your self and the manner you use, and additionally primarily based totally totally on some detail life comes to a decision to throw at you. Be organized. This is why you need to be constantly reviewing your desires and rate range, no longer first-rate due to the reality you're trying to stay heading inside the right direction, however because of the fact that music may also trade on you, whether or not or now not you have a look at it coming or now not. The greater you can prepare for what's to come back lower back, the greater without problems you could react in a manner that blessings you.

Say "No"

As tough as this could be to three, especially folks who're simply beginning out residing on a price range, you're going to need to get snug with saying the phrases, "It's now not in the budget." Living on a budget can regularly feel like we're dwelling negative or as a minimum in a way this is constricted. We may additionally moreover, at instances, sense left out socially, or enjoy like others might be pitying us. At instances like the ones, it's essential to preserve in thoughts those information of what the common American goes thru financially. Your social circle is most in all likelihood going via the equal struggles as you are. You, however, have decided on to do some thing proactive and realistic about it. You're no longer budgeting because you're horrible; you're budgeting, due to the reality you've got goals and are financially accountable.

Remember the test in now not on time gratification? This is likewise a 2nd for you to test your potential to face up to impulse purchases and splurges in trade for the assurance that your destiny can be wealthier in truth because you selected to stand as much as wasteful spending in recent times. Be willing to look ahead to some thing better.

Have Enthusiasm for Your Goals

In continuing with the exercise of now not on time gratification, keeping your eyes for your prize is lots easier when you're enthusiastic about your goals. Before you start executing or perhaps making plans your budget, you may want to take the time to certainly determine what your financial independence absolutely technique to you. What does it suggest to be unfastened collectively with your coins? What do you sense due to being unfastened? What does a day of financial independence look like for you? From there, you may definitely get unique approximately what it is you need, further to how a extremely good deal it'll price.

After that, get visible! Put photographs of your dreams in your fridge, for your toilet reflect, or to your automobile. Create a vision board in case you actually need to have amusing with it. Have a easy declaration of your goals for your budgeting sheet or pocket ebook. If you're the usage of an app for keeping song of your fee variety, then attempt developing a profile image or history photograph that has to do collectively along with your desires if you could. Cover your report folders with photographs of adventure places or the destiny college of your choice. Give your on-line spreadsheets names that remind you of your various goals.

Imagine that financially free day: How do you revel in whilst you wake up inside the morning? What are your plans for that day? What do you get to do, have, provide? As corny as visualizing can sound, this isn't about wishful wondering. Seeing what you need in your thoughts's eye brings what you are doing nowadays into consciousness.

Only Increase Spending When...

Increasing your spending energy is probably clever only whilst you're without a doubt out of debt and on the right track in your savings dreams. You have a good way to relaxation assured which you don't want to rely upon any form of credit at the manner to live within the manner you need. If you find out your self typically going again to credit gambling cards for the fundamental gadgets to your costs list, you then're maximum probably no longer prepared to improve your manner of existence.

In the upcoming chapters, we'll be going over debt manipulate and cash mindsets, and without any form of stable footing in the ones regions, you'll generally discover yourself struggling with coins. More cash isn't going to solve each hassle, and, in fact, the extra cash you've got were given were given, the more problems you'll create in case you don't learn how to manipulate the coins you already do own.

Financial Literacy

When higher, you do better. –Dr. Maya Angelou

During your allotted time for budgeting each week or , spend a similarly 20 or half of of-hour gaining knowledge of a cutting-edge financial expertise or concept. Had all of us had a chunk literacy on non-public finance in immoderate faculty, it might be stable to mention that the middle-income families of North America might not find themselves inside the positions they'll be in these days. Lack of know-how in making an investment, a dense manner of lifestyles spherical the usage of credit gambling cards, the ever-developing hazard of scholar loan debt... Had we had a higher education spherical our very very own budget, it might be that budgeting could be 2d nature to clearly every body.

Expanding your information round your very non-public rate range is an empowering practice that could help you to keep away from pricey and prolonged-term errors, as well as assist you take reputedly daunting financial steps with greater self guarantee. Honing your skills in this location can only assist you build your wealth that masses faster.

Chapter 8: Debt Management

Many oldsters commonly don't realize how crucial our relationship with credit score rating rating is until once we've made a large mistake with it. Having an tremendous credit score rating score can determine how quickly you get a automobile loan or how with out problems you get authorized for a mortgage. Your credit score score score can also even determine how loads credit score you get authorized for on credit rating playing cards or lines of credit score. Basically, if your rating is low, you're likely to get small credit score score limit quantities, if any in any respect. Your statistics with credit score score may additionally even determine what kinds of hobby prices loaners at monetary institutions are willing to offer you. The poorer your relationship with credit rating, the greater hobby you'll want to pay if you do get authorized.

If you're well into your adulthood, you then definately apprehend via manner of now debt control is a few thing to get in the the front of. Most North Americans, but, are unfortunately drowning in it, making the trouble of dealing with rate variety all the greater intimidating and disheartening. The reality of the problem is that there's no person coming to prevent and erase all of your beyond mistakes; you're going to want to study what's going on collectively collectively along with your coins and cope with it. So, if it's no longer going to be painless, how can we at the least make this as effective and inexperienced as we are able to?

Facing Down Your Debt

Debt is particularly discouraging, as it method the cash that you're strolling for these days and the foreseeable destiny is going towards topics that already befell. These are purchases you've made within the beyond that you could or may not even bear in mind, so it appears like your tough-earned bucks are going to the financial group or group that gave you the credit score card. Additionally, with the hobby they charge, you're going to probably pay 40%—60% greater at the object you placed for your credit score card than you may've, had you paid coins.

Take a take a look at some of your credit score rating rating card purchases: Do you remember taking element in them? Were they well nicely really worth the hobby paid and the extra hours spent walking to pay them off? You have to've likewise decided no one of a kind preference in using credit score score at the same time as confronted with a dire financial emergency. How precious may an emergency account were at that point? These are hard inquiries to face, but the way you cope with your reactions to them will decide what sorts of economic moves you are making going ahead. Do you continue to bury your head in the sand, or do you placed your head down and get to work?

Your debt can be why you discover art work so drab and lengthy. The interest itself isn't usually what's keeping you below a cloud, but it's the fact that you're running and not the use of a destiny dreams to hold your spirit up and endorsed. Everything you work for is going to a person you owe, so rather

165

than you taking proactive steps inside the path of your destiny, it's as an alternative not on time further and in addition.

With your budgeting recreation plan, but, this is your possibility to provide you with a systematic plan that could assist you get a deal with of what's absolutely taking region and the way effective you're being. Rather than simply throwing coins at your debt month after month, a plan will will let you see wherein your cash is being wasted or not growing a dent at all! You want to be extra conscientious about what amount of cash goes in which, and with hobby, hidden prices, and so on; you may be amazed to discover simply how useless your money is. Our cause with this bankruptcy is to help you find out the holes for your price variety, so that you can then learn how to plug them up. Getting a handle to your expenses no longer fine manner lots much less waste, but it additionally method unclutching yourself out of your dependence on credit.

Keeping Your Credit in Check

If you need to decorate your dating with credit score that permits you to appearance a piece extra notable to creditors from numerous economic establishments, then you definitely in reality've had been given to pay extra interest for your credit score rating. There are a few factors which you cannot have concept of as a way to have an impact on your credit rating. We may not had been taught approximately these factors in university, and the humans promoting credit score score gambling playing cards really don't element out them, however they're key in growing the right behavior whilst coping with borrowed coins.

The Due Date

Getting within the dependancy of lacking due dates doesn't maintain nicely in your credit score rating. In truth, left out payments can display up to your report as a ways once more as 36 months and could play a function in determining your credit score rating rating rating. How you use your credit rating score cards money owed for 60%—70% of the manner your score is decided. That is to say, it's now not sufficient that you have a low stability or a minimal amount of debt. If you don't have proper conduct approximately paying your payments on-time, this will have your credit rating rating plummeting south.

Paying on time isn't simplest about your credit score rating, but moreover approximately how hundreds time you spend in debt. The more late charges you may incur genuinely with the beneficial aid of taking too lengthy, no longer most effective approach having more money come out of your pocket, however it technique greater months spent not taking steps towards your dreams and financial freedom. Think of every month that you've ignored a rate as two or 3 months down the street that you want to eliminate getting what you honestly need. We will, on common, pay an extra $2,000 in hobby fees on a $three,000 balance. So, without a doubt recall what it's miles you're shopping for along facet your credit rating card; you might wind up paying double for it!

The Minimum Payment

Paying the minimum charge on all of your loans is another essential behavioral aspect to maintaining the ones money owed in suitable popularity. Paying underneath the minimum of what's required or not paying in any respect indicates the reality which you cannot be able to handling what it's miles which you borrowed. This is a few special hit to the credit rating score and will cause costs as nicely. If you find out you're suffering with the minimal necessities that the financial institution has installation, you may want to try contacting them to barter some other affiliation. If your credit rating rating is top notch, and you've continually been in proper standing with the enterprise, they is probably willing to negotiate a plan that would assist you meet your monthly obligations. A lot of establishments may want to as an alternative every sports art work some aspect out as opposed to no longer pay attention from you the least bit. They'd as an opportunity be open to a ultra-modern plan than be uncertain of whether or not or no longer or not they'll be getting a number of their cash again this month.

Remember past due, disregarded, or insufficient payments are elements in your detail which will have an effect in your credit score rating more than something else. Creditors are seeking to look the manner you behave with credit rating as a manner to then determine what you may get going forward.

Create a Bill Payment Calendar

This element of keeping your credit score rating rating in test is exactly what it looks as if. Having the whole lot on price range becomes extra effective while every object is time-touchy. This guarantees you get everything finished and paid in complete on-time, and at the same time as you've set up your plan, you don't want to keep in mind it overly masses afterward.

Depending on how a bargain of a difficulty debt rate is for your finances, you may want first of all it first, or 2nd in case you've made a dedication to pay yourself first each month. The first element to do is take inventory of all your minimum bills and precisely whilst every one of them is due. It is probably a extraordinary idea to pick a separate account out of your one in every of a type everyday economic organization debts particular strictly for debt compensation. Depending on at the same time as you gets a fee every month, you'll fill the account due to this, after which have the important debt payments set up to come out robotically from that account. If it's possible, try to have the ones bills robotically debit a few days earlier to make sure no overdue bills and, therefore, no more fees.

Are Your Funds Limited This Month?

Do you locate your price range is tight this month, and also you're really no longer going if you need to satisfy your payments? If this is the case, it's awesome to fulfill the minimum payments of prolonged-repute payments that have usually been in proper order and to in all likelihood take the hit on your credit score rating rating through lacking or developing a late price to an account that's both new or already rocky. This is because of credit score information which we'll talk a bit greater approximately later. You could possibly count on that paying a chunk bit inside the path of every debt, in spite of the reality that meaning coming brief of the minimum on they all, is better than not some thing. You run the risk, although, of putting an account that's usually been healthy in a bad way. Having more than one or all of your credit rating loans in terrible reputation is worse than having absolutely one or .

Building Good Credit and Avoiding Debt

Knowing this understanding, whether or not or now not or not you have already got debt (in accurate reputation or in any other case), or are genuinely seeking to have your first credit score rating rating card or take out your first mortgage, it's important to apprehend precisely what it way to use credit score correctly. This is the distinction among drowning in debt years down the road, and the use of the wave with manipulate. Whether you've got small balances or address big loans, you could experience assured that you commonly recognize the way to make it back to shore.

Obstacles

Having a awful credit score rating is a critical issue in determining whether or not or now not or not you get accepted for a mortgage. This isn't surely a depend of having the credit score score card you'd like, however this will furthermore be a figuring out component in how lots credit score you'll be eligible to get. You may be denied a car or home, because of a awful statistics with credit. Getting a cope with on your debt now in preference to setting it off will prevent you from sinking similarly.

Waiting need to have you ever ever ever walking the risk of getting thus far deep that you find out yourself trying help from collections and financial catastrophe businesses. While this may be a viable answer for hundreds, this isn't a smooth preserve in mind of getting someone help you deal with your debt. A lot of the time, the ones types of groups can keep your one of a kind property as collateral. Should some issue occur, they keep the proper to capture some thing you've got were given have been given or block you from having access to it altogether. On the other hand, a economic wreck, at the same time as wiping the slate smooth so to speak, places you in a completely slim function financially. You can lose numerous property similar to the equity in your house or positive investment belongings which you've made. Your monetary break may also stay for your credit score record for up to seven years. All of those factors depend on your personal document and the agreement you're making with the organisation you decide to art work with. However, it's crucial to preserve this stuff in thoughts whilst thinking about your debt. The longer you wait to face it and address it, the more likely you'll locate your self attempting assist from a collections or financial catastrophe company. Get a manipulate for your debt earlier than it gets to that aspect!

Only Borrow What You Can Afford to Pay Off

Using a credit card isn't approximately being able to buy matters you could't otherwise discover the coins for once you've paid all your special expenses. If this is the case for you, you'll want to take a vital have a study your way of lifestyles. Credit playing cards have made all of it too smooth for max human beings to start dwelling best a touch bit outside of our way. When you start to depend on your credit rating rating to live your current way of lifestyles, you run the threat of completing in a situation like we simply stated within the very last section.

When getting non-public loans or a credit rating card, be careful of the limits that the financial establishments are presenting you. Just due to the fact they've deemed you certified to have a super restriction, doesn't propose you need to take it. When going for walks with credit score rating score, clearly take into account what it's miles that you need and why, not what your monetary organization is willing to provide you and what number of allowances they'll make. Your dating collectively along with your credit score rating score is among you and you. A fashionable rule of thumb while the usage of your credit score score card is to decide if you could without problems pay off the object you're buying with the resource of the surrender of the month. If you could repay the balance of your card by way of the stop of the month, then it's appropriate enough to use your credit rating card. You in fact may also pick to use it, due to the truth you'd as an alternative no longer wait till your next paycheck to get the item. Using your credit score score card can be beneficial for payments like your cell smartphone or internet bill. You'll want to pay the ones objects except, and this is a manner to exercise use of your credit score score score in a way that permits improve your rating.

Your Credit Limit vs Your Credit Balance

While we're with reference to credit limits, there's every other problem that would gravely have an effect on your credit score score score rating: How masses of your restriction do you use on a regular foundation? Having constantly maxed out credit rating card limits will adversely have an effect on your rating. A wholesome tip to keep in mind is which you need to preserve your stability underneath 30%—40% of your restrict usually. Again, in spite of the reality that you have were given a sure restrict, doesn't recommend you want to apply it all, and be given as proper with it or not, your credit score file can be tormented by how a great deal making a decision to use. Ironically enough, whether or not or no longer or not you operate the entire amount of your restrict, you're although chargeable for the whole quantity, and it's factored into your liabilities even in case your stability is way underneath it.

That being said, you have to truly do not forget why you are getting a credit rating card and set up location sure behavioral barriers for your self if you sense your spending would possibly probably get out of hand. To upload to the irony, a person who offers most effective in coins and doesn't have a records of credit score rating the least bit can be grew to end up away for industrial agency loans or a loan irrespective of the fact they've typically paid for the whole lot in full and have assets. With no history of credit score score, creditors can't recognize the way you'd fare with their loaned cash. Since we find out ourselves in a world that does function on credit score score score to a positive volume, the use of credit score will make a whole lot of of factors greater accessible for you. However, getting to know a manner to use it well in order that it doesn't get out of hand is vital.

History Actually Matters

Another detail of maintaining a regularly immoderate credit rating rating has to do with facts. It's not a thing this is obvious, however it makes sense to creditors that you maintaining a credit score score score card account or a private loan for an prolonged time body displays your skills of staying disciplined lengthy-time period. In exclusive phrases, a long and fantastic records suggests which you've usually been someone with the proper conduct. Lenders are inside the business employer of loaning coins, due to the truth they are capable of make coins from the hobby they fee. Having an account in relevant fame that's been open for a long term is what they're seeking out in a person they will mortgage to.

If you do have an vintage credit rating score card account which you've been death to dispose of, you might want to count on once more. You may additionally have set your thoughts on relieving yourself of this card for a long term, however bear in thoughts virtually getting it all the way right down to a balance of zero alternatively. What you need to artwork on next is your courting with this credit score card. It may also moreover have for a long time seemed similar to the thorn on your element, but do not forget the reality that feeling out of manage collectively along with your coins or unsure of your self financially is what delivered about your risky feelings from the start. Consider retaining the lengthy-reputation credit score rating card, specially if you sense you sooner or later have a deal with in your rate variety and debt, and if you now feel a whole lot less susceptible to impulse spending.

Using Your Credit Cards Responsibly

We all realize we want to use our credit score score playing cards responsibly, however if we're being sincere with ourselves, lots people didn't find out about these most not unusual factors which have an effect on a wonderful credit score rating score in advance than. Should cash management, tax overall performance, and credit rating score health be subjects we examine in college? Yes, possibly, but due to the reality that they aren't (or, at the least, now not to a significant volume), the super we are capable of do is to study those education through a bit of trial and errors. If you live vigilant and proactive, you'll decrease that margin for mistakes by using manner of manner of a protracted shot, retaining greater of your very own bucks in your pocket.

What Is My Credit Card Really For?

If we're dealing with our coins healthily and capable of live interior our technique, then realistically speaking credit score rating score wouldn't be of use to us! Except for situations wherein we'd want big loans for a loan, or a automobile, or perhaps to begin a commercial company, in which case a high-quality credit score information would be beneficial. Our tradition of intake and overspending, but, has all began to embody credit score score into its budget as a way to useful resource a manner of life. This is definitely now not what credit score rating is for!

If you're going to apply a credit score rating card, permit or no longer it is sincerely to build up and maintain a notable score, no longer for purchasing belongings you wouldn't be able to have enough money in any other case. Choose some routine fees to be located in your credit score score card that you want to pay anyway. Then, have your monetary institution account be routinely drafted to that credit score rating card quick after to pay down the stability. This manner, you're the use of up your credit score rating regularly and successfully while not having to reflect onconsideration on it an excessive amount of. If you're genuinely tempted to buy some factor out of price variety, actually motive with your self the realities of making the purchase. How lengthy will you wind up finding out to shop for this object, and is it simply really worth the more money you'll pay for it in interest?

What Kind of Card Should I Get?

If you've been fortunate enough to find out this e-book earlier than having gotten your first credit score score rating card, you then need to examine out for high-quality types of cards before you are making a dedication to genuinely each person. Always search for low hobby credit score rating playing cards, which you could typically discover at a financial organization. Have you ever had a salesperson approach you at a shop looking to sell you their preserve's "top fee membership" card or a few component of that nature? While there can be a completely appealing praise tool to using this card for purchases, pretty some the time these hold credit score rating playing playing cards are well-known for having a number of the excellent costs of hobby. It's without a doubt top notch to keep away from getting the kind of. While the rewards they marketplace it can be very attractive, they're capable of make such gives of free in-keep gadgets or present gambling cards while you rack up factors, because they're overcharging you in fees and hobby within the first location. At the give up of the day, they're simply genuinely paying you yet again the coins they overcharged you initially. Pay interest to the shape of agreement you're getting: The a lot less tough, the better. This manner, you'll be precipitated to hold your non-public use of the cardboard clean and minimum as properly.

How Should I Use My Perks?

If you do have a rewards or coins-lower returned element for your credit score score card, it's no longer all awful. You just need to make sure the hobby you're paying is definitely nicely really worth it for you. With this, you'd ought to do a chunk of calculating. Measure your interest paid as opposed to the rewards or cash you'd get lower once more. This is as clean as going over your statements every month to peer how masses in prices have been charged to your account. Then, check what you get in pass returned. This might certainly be beneficial if you could spend that money once more on property you're purchasing for besides. This may be beneficial in saving you some extra greenbacks, and it's similar to your mother and father said, "Every little bit counts!" You can also use any gift playing cards or certificates you've earned through your specific rewards software program program to your entertainment and amusement elegance. In fact, that is probably part of your rate variety, in that you don't in reality budget your earnings on the way to encompass a leisure and entertainment phase, but with whatever you've earned for your rewards software, you preserve mainly and strictly for fun subjects!

www.ingramcontent.com/pod-product-compliance
Lightning Source LLC
Chambersburg PA
CBHW071218210326
41597CB00016B/1857